The Poetry Beat

Poets on Poetry   Donald Hall, General Editor

Tom Clark

The Poetry Beat

REVIEWING THE EIGHTIES

Ann Arbor
The University of Michigan Press

1993   1992   1991   1990   4   3   2   1

Library of Congress Cataloging-in-Publication Data

The poetry beat : reviewing the eighties / [compiled by] Tom Clark.
        p.   cm.—(Poets on poetry)
     ISBN 0-472-09428-9 (alk. paper).—ISBN 0-472-06428-2
(pbk. : alk. paper)
     1. American poetry—20th century—History and criticism.
  2. English poetry—History and criticism.   3. Poetry—Book
  reviews.
  I. Clark, Tom, 1941–   .   II. Series.
  PS325.P58   1990
  811'.509—dc20   90-11059
                                                              CIP

Preface

Although I was trained in good schools to be a scholar and critic, I never actually attained the elevated station of Professorhood. Some twenty-odd years ago, I found myself thrown back on my education combined with whatever I had left by way of natural resources, as I attempted to make a living as a free-lance writer. It has been a long and sometimes grubby adventure. Over this past decade, the surviving flicker of an early interest in poetry has caused me to spend a good deal of time writing about new books of verse for newspapers, mostly in California. Often the books I have written about were chosen by others (editors), a factor that has no doubt expanded the extent if at times thinned the depths of my interests. Often, again due to the venue, these pieces' previous appearances have come in forms variously mutated by editorial oversight if not also by the sheer mischance of typos. Here, at long last, is the pure and unadulterated product—the reviews as I wrote them, in the original state as typed up after being scribbled in extra fine point 0.3 millimeter Express pens on the backs of my daughter's school homework, my night school students' poems, and my own recycled manuscripts.

Given the large and miscellaneous quality of the potential audience—that of a big-city Sunday newspaper, a far cry from that conglomeration of small coteries we know of as the "poetry audience"—not much could be taken for granted in writing these reviews, and certain background data of a historical and biographical nature had necessarily to be supplied. Though to some this information may seem frivolous (or even embarrassingly obvious), I find in looking over the pieces again now that the fragmentary life-gossip about poets may be the most interesting thing in them. "The biographical part of literature is what I love the most," said Samuel Johnson, even before he'd embarked on his *Lives*. I suspect a lot of us who consider ourselves interested in literature would be lying if we didn't confess to agreement.

With such a collection as this, of course, there is always the question, "Why publish a bunch of old reviews?" The short answer is: a lot of these books seem for one reason or another never to have received more extensive (or in some cases *any*) attention elsewhere. Still, qualms about republication linger. Thinking again of Dr. Johnson, the literary journalist par excellence, we know he took small pride or pleasure from his journalistic accomplishment, leaving little doubt that he felt rueful about attaching his name to it. A contemporary reported that when asked well afterward by friends to reveal the dates of his early appearances in the *Gentleman's Magazine* and elsewhere (so that they could go look them up), the great critic declined in embarrassment. To others he acknowledged that in his journalistic career he had in fact written "many things which merited no distinction from the trash with which they were consigned to oblivion." Much of this occasional criticism, as Johnson's biographer Walter J. Bate suggests, was indeed hack work, but hack work of a sometimes inspired kind. The occasion may have been momentary but the mind at work was still Johnson's. That can't of course be said of what follows here.

Contents

Cabaret of Despair

"We poets in our youth begin in gladness; but thereof comes in the end despondency and madness." So wrote William Wordsworth on the premature death of the eighteenth-century poet, Thomas Chatterton.

Unhappy fate made Sylvia Plath's life an instance of the truth of Wordsworth's dictum—although for her "the end" followed too closely on the beginning, without any middle. She had been writing seriously for only about seven years when she died by her own hand in 1963, at the age of thirty-one, after predicting her death in a brilliant and morbidly gripping series of poems.

The confessional aspect of these last poems, whose intimate tone and startling, obsessive imagery frankly reflected her personal alienation and anguish, unfortunately made Plath's work into a posthumous spectacle for popular consumption, and her life into a touchstone "case" provoking widespread gossip, both literary and psychological. *Ariel*, a book of her late poetry, sold 270,000 copies, many of them to people who hadn't previously bought a poetry book, and who haven't bought one since.

By an odd irony, popular success did not exactly ensure Plath's poems a place in the literary pantheon. Rather, it obscured their value. The sensational aspects of the *Ariel* poems, and the largely uncritical mass attention they received, almost blinded one to their strengths and small weak-

Review of *The Collected Poems* by Sylvia Plath, edited by Ted Hughes, *San Francisco Chronicle,* 1981.

nesses—the musical and imagistic genius, and the occasionally excessive self-absorption.

It's now possible to examine this work in the more temperate light of history, thanks to the editorial efforts of Plath's husband, British poet Ted Hughes, who has here arranged 224 Plath poems—all she wrote, says Hughes, between her twenty-third and thirty-first years—into chronological order. He also provides an appendix with useful notes and a liberal selection of juvenilia.

In her early poems of the fifties, gifted but polite exercises in the verse of the period, it's easy to detect the glittering formal skills that made Plath a good poet, but not the power that made her into a nearly great one. That came later, in the "despondency and madness" of 1962–63.

In those years, Plath's formal skills were reaching a peak, but they were in the service of internal disorder. Out of a state of extreme tension she conceived distracting image thickets, forests of anxiety. The poetry becomes a cabaret of despair, the poems small self-disclosing psycho-dramatic monologues—chatty, allusive, self-mocking, full of casually disarming shockers ("Daddy, I have had to kill you"), staggering in slow gestural cadences, or tripping along on the raw nerve-ending lilt of singsong children's rhymes. It's original writing and then some, outdistancing its influences (e.g., Robert Lowell) and sometimes achieving a kind of ductile intensity, with the heat of the imagination flowing through the images like a direct current that melts and re-fuses them, creating patterns of multiple, shifting meaning.

All this is enhanced in *The Collected Poems* by the ongoing narrative interest of Hughes's notes and his day-by-day chronological dating of the poems, which indicate whole "phases" of Plath's late writing compressed into the space of weeks and even days.

"The blood jet is poetry, / There is no stopping it," she wrote a few weeks before her death. Indeed, as the poems move down to the chilling conclusion of "The Edge," an impersonal vision of suicide, there is a sense that the poet's demise is not only foretold, but demanded, by her poetry—as if in taking her own life she were merely living out (or living up to) the macabre destiny spelled out by her images. "Fixed stars / Govern a life," she wrote. "The woman is perfected. / Her dead / Body wears the smile of accomplishment."

Keeping the dizzying account of this fatal spin was an exercise in artistic control, like handling a speeding racing car. Ironically, the challenge sharpened Plath's powers, made her a better driver in the final laps.

Highballs and Breakdowns

This is a book about an exclusive group of poets whose works and presences dominated the postwar American poetic establishment: John Berryman, Robert Lowell, Delmore Schwartz, Randall Jarrell & co.

When I was a youthful aspirant to poetry-writing myself, some twenty-five years ago, these poets were the giants of the scene—or anyway of its academic suburbs, where all the publicity was.

And what publicity! An aura of self-destruction (or self-indulgence) hung over the whole group like a black halo as they spun out a verse that distilled the drawing-room angst of an entire generation of educated, liberal, brilliant, drinking neurotics. The fifties and early sixties stock of "Lowell stories," alone, would fill a book. Lowell and Berryman were renowned as the champion nihilist drunks of an age in which, it seemed, you couldn't be a real poet without alternating highballs and Miltowns, having constant breakdowns, fearing and envying all your contemporaries; being obsessed with the Virgin Mary and experiencing stigmata, or going around with one foot out the window, threatening to jump.

My favorite Lowell story, while we're at it, is one told me by Robert Frost in 1962. Frost was then respected as poetic elder of the land (Ezra Pound was in exile and William Carlos Williams was not yet regarded seriously in the Establishment). "The last time I saw Cal Lowell," Frost told me, "was at a party. He was drunk and spent a long time lying on the floor pour-

Review of *Poets in Their Youth: A Memoir* by Eileen Simpson, *San Francisco Chronicle,* 1982.

ing drinks on his face. I told him to get up, for heaven's sake. He did; but he then proceeded to pin me against a wall, lift me up by my lapels, and in an awful voice, with his chin in my face, he said, 'who's a better poet, me or Dick Wilbur?' "

At any rate, one looks back now at this group and their agonies, which grow colder year by year on the pages of their books, with lingering if diminishing respect, and perhaps a growing impatience. Were they really, as the blurb for this book claims, "America's most important poets since Pound and Eliot"? Or were they merely elegant masters of a dying mode, talented certainly but seriously limited in outlook, range and ability to engage readers outside a small, trained academic circle?

This is a question of aesthetic value that's understandably begged in the interesting personal memoir by Eileen Simpson, a novelist and psychotherapist who was the wife of John Berryman from 1942 to 1953.

Simpson does little to explain why, despite the eminence and success of their literary careers, these poets were so crippled in their private lives by alcoholism, marital problems and mental instability. All of the principals of Simpson's story are dead now, prematurely; Berryman leapt to his death from a bridge, Simpson implies that Randall Jarrell's death was also a suicide, and others in the group died indirectly from the effects of booze. Perhaps the cause was an illness that was cultural as well as psychological.

But *Poets in Their Youth* is a memoir, not a case study. Simpson does offer one general observation: Lowell, Schwartz, Berryman, along with their older colleague Richard Blackmur, all went through unhappy childhoods, "torn between a powerful mother and an ineffectual father." Berryman's father, for instance, committed suicide at age thirty-nine, an event which, Simpson claims, left the poet permanently scarred.

After surviving their various childhood traumas, these poets shared in adulthood a common egocentricity. While this may have facilitated their confessional verse, it certainly aggravated their personal lives, as Simpson shows. "Making it" as a poet in America is usually the result of considerable ambition, and doesn't come without its price in interior turmoil.

By the 1950s, the writers to whom marriage had introduced Eileen Simpson had become the leading literary lights of the time. They played musical chairs with the best academic positions, danced at the Stork Club and spent convivial evenings together in each other's comfortable homes, drinking and exchanging literary gossip.

Gradually, though, the urbane veneer began to show cracks. Simpson demonstrates, through various episodes, how the youthful enthusiasm folded up in middle age, becoming a general neurotic anxiety. The elegant evenings, one by one, turn into unpleasant scenes. At a party hosted by Saul Bellow, a drunken Delmore Schwartz disrupts the dancing, accusing his wife of flirting, and is only prevented from beating her up by the intercession of John Berryman. Robert Lowell, while resident at Yaddo writers' retreat, has a nervous breakdown, during which he first launches an anticommunist attack on some of his associates, and then calls up all his friends to ask them "to hear the will of God."

In Allen Ginsberg's circle, none of this might have seemed so horrible—in fact, it'd probably have been regarded as amusing—but in the big-time Establishment, it was very bad behavior, indeed, and a public embarrassment.

Simpson takes her title from Wordsworth, whom Delmore Schwartz liked to quote: "We poets in our youth begin in gladness; / But thereof comes in the end despondency and madness." (Schwartz, she tells us, used to substitute the word *sadness* for Wordsworth's "gladness.")

Although elegiac in tone, *Poets in Their Youth* is a tender rather than a gloomy book. Another author might have sensationalized the suicides, infidelities and mental illnesses which ravaged these poets' lives. But Eileen Simpson, avoiding such obvious pitfalls, writes with grace, dignity and genteel restraint. Salvaging many moments worth saving from the "rotten life" Delmore Schwartz predicted would be her fate for marrying a poet, she adds a new perspective on this group of poets who are looking more and more, as the years pass, like their own "lost" generation, less notable for what they achieved than for what they may have thrown away.

These Tropics Aren't Triste

I never met Victor Cruz but I like his sense of irony, which is very subtle yet powerfully lucid. Irony in writing isn't an easy quality to pick up because it requires you to mask your delivery, like throwing a changeup in baseball—you have to "take something off the pitch." If your motion is too obvious, it won't work. The art of indirection depends on giving a convincing imitation of doing one thing while you're actually doing something else.

An example of this is Cruz's prose poem to some low-riding modern-day caballeros, the Watsonville Road Kings, who glide from Mission Street to "T.J." (Tijuana) on "El Camino Irreal," a road "the state of California made for us," in a "full fleet of 20 cars."

Their caballos are metal. It doesn't matter to them "if the manufacturer was Ford or General Motors," because what counts is not the original model but the styling, which is as personal as the riders' souls—and involves things like chrome, velvet, and the silky vocals of Smokey Robinson cooing "Oo Baby" over Pioneer speakers. "When the metal is yours you put your mark on it, buying something is only the first step, what you do to it is your name, your history of angles." Cruz's Road Kings make their customized cars their living rooms, in a weird architectural enjambment of "Gothic mixed with Toltecas."

In the middle of the Road Kings' power glide to T.J., though, Cruz changes speeds on us. The "Low Writer," or author, does some ironic styling of his own, which changes the

Review of *By Lingual Wholes* by Victor Hernandez Cruz, *San Francisco Chronicle*, 1982.

heroic naturalism of his piece into something else. "But wait," he implores the riders, "how long will this oil supply last . . . you cannot replace it like coffee or tobacco . . . the blood of the earth once it's taken out leaves space." The Road Kings, in their hungry Detroit combustion boxes, don't replenish what they burn up, and so leave behind them only another one of those "holes" Cruz writes so much about—this one full of nothing.

This ironic collision of values—the romance of low-riding vs. the diminution of planetary resources—is really a mini-clash between poetry and "realistic" practicality. Cruz resolves it by letting poetry momentarily fly up over the practical world as only it can. "When the gasoline stops pumping," he suggests, "the vehicles will run on perfume and music." Customized soulfully, they're no longer mere Detroit iron but "butterflies with transmissions," existing beyond the depreciable earth in a dimension of pure style.

But don't get the impression from all this talk of "irony" and "values" that these densely flowering urban jungle poems are classroom-sleepy. Victor Cruz's tropics aren't triste. On white pages, they turn red and green and yellow from sheer metaphorical heat. Cruz can write with an angel on his arm, a bird in his ear, a woman in his heart and history on his mind, make it all come out sadly funny or beautiful and still walk down the street smiling.

This collection's punning title is multiply suggestive; its meanings pervade the book. Holes, dots and zeros—universal symbols which can "become everything in the world"—crop up in work after work. So does the idea—or ideal—of "bilingual wholes." Ideal is matched by performance; Cruz indeed creates something as close to a seamless, bilingual lyric voice as one can imagine, weaving English and Spanish not only into the same poems but often into the same lines.

It's an adventurous attempt that works, because Cruz has a sureness of music that can only be natural. By strange accident of biography, he takes his place in a tradition of "English" which is twice removed from his roots: he was born in Puerto Rico, grew up on the Lower East Side of New York, but is wise enough to recognize that "if I lived in older times /

With a funny name like Choicer or / Henry Howard, Earl of Surrey, what chimes! / I would spend my times in search of rhymes."

If his discrimination of ear is ancient ("the Island of Puerto Rico / is the ears of Saru-Saru, a poet reported to have lived / in Atlantis"), the pacing of his work is modern, post-bop, post-rock, post-salsa—not a "minuet slow" but a "*mambo* of much more haste," or sometimes a *merengue* that "vibrates more than a mambo by about 30 percent." When he slows down, it's not to walk but to take up the sinuous movements of "the bolero, the ballade, the fish, the grind." This is poetry with an asphalt-bred choreography nimble enough to state its anti-colonialism in a quick pivot between steps and stoops: "Ponce de Leon knew that to be truly successful he'd have to ban feet."

Camping among the Shades

From the First Nine is a calm, cool collection of poems by a fifty-six-year-old now regarded as an American master—critical favorite of East Coast academicians, winner (twice) of National Book Awards, recipient of Pulitzer and Bollingen prizes.

The early work in this book dates back to James Merrill's twentieth year. Even in youth, he seems to have possessed the polish of a mature practitioner. Perfection, in fact, hung around Merrill's literary reputation from the first. To his natural gifts as a poet—a bright, active mind, a dry whimsy, a sense of versification quick as a cat's glance and an innate sensitivity to poetry as music, its luxuries and conceits—was added the presumed social advantage of having the blue blood of the patrician in his veins.

It seemed to vivify his poems as well. Merrill wrote at first in an exquisite, meditative style, taking his tone from W. H. Auden and his conception from Wallace Stevens, contriving elegant, artifice-laden lyrics, remote in diction, but following the Romantics in subject: These were essentially poems about art, inspiration, imagination.

Several of the earlier poems are, indeed, almost perfect. One is tempted to pick out "Angel" (first published in a 1962 collection)—partly because it is one of the most brilliantly achieved of Merrill's works; partly because it marks a transition to the witty, relaxed, more expansively colloquial poetry that came later; and partly because it is the debut of Merrill's angel-figure, the admonitory herald or messenger from an-

---

Review of *From the First Nine: Poems 1946–1976* and *The Changing Light at Sandover* by James Merrill, *San Francisco Chronicle*, 1983.

other dimension, who later became his controlling symbol. The angel who arrives in Merrill's poem, "demanding praise, demanding surrender," is a relative of the classic muse (a being invoked by and for poetry) and a literary descendant also of the angel in Rainer Maria Rilke's *Duino Elegies.*

The invocation of ultra-dimensional beings, some of whose power and knowledge would hopefully transmit itself in the verse, became Merrill's principal poetic pursuit in the middle 1970s, when he began making poems about his long experience with spirit-raising and table-tapping. In these poems, Merrill's use of ouija-board iterations (which are professed, in the poems, to be literal) is a device for contacting "higher" realms of being and thus ascending, jacob's-ladder-style, beyond the limits of mortality—against which romantic poetry, with its worship of "inspiration," perennially surges.

With his "topsy turvy" teacup pointer—a willow-ware cup "waltzing on an alphabet board"—Merrill summons his first being-from-beyond in "The Will" (first published in 1976), the strongest long poem in *From the First Nine.* Here the ethereal guest places upon the poet a sacred duty: "SET MY TEACHINGS DOWN . . . IF U DO NOT YR WORLD WILL BE UNDONE." This imperative tone spills over into Merrill's first two book-length ouija-board poems, "The Book of Ephraim" and "Mirabell" (both contained in *The Changing Light at Sandover*), where the poet demonstrates his willingness to "GIVE UP EVERYTHING EXCEPT THE GHOST" in order to transcribe the dictations of his other-dimensional visitors. His first major "contact" is Ephraim, a first-century Greek put to death on Capri in 36 A.D. for being the lover of Caligula.

Dead poets (Auden, Stevens), dead friends and relatives also appear, speaking in ALL-CAPS telegraphese. With the arrival of Mirabell, a "fallen" archangel (one of the "winged men" from a period "B4 MANKIND") who appoints Merrill his "scribe," the work takes a metaphysical turn. In speeches of some vision and profundity, Mirabell "dictates" the history of earth and mankind, including the incarnation and withdrawal of "God Biology"—a supreme being whose power buckled with the splitting of the atom by Enrico Fermi in 1934. From this point the "Book of Mirabell" becomes, as

Merrill half-jokingly suggests, "warmed-up Milton, Dante, Genesis"—an attempt to update *Paradise Lost* in contemporary ghost-language.

It's a stirring effort, but there are problems. First, no matter how light the touch, poets writing about séances may court the sublime, but never hover far from the brink of the ridiculous—as witness W. B. Yeats's *A Vision*. More serious, perhaps, are problems of keeping a narrative going. Everybody in Merrill's ouija-board poems is either dead, preoccupied with death, or was never alive in the first place. Much of the poems' scant action takes place in the ghost heralds' oracular dictations. Because of Merrill's use of typographical signals (wide margins for the "angels," LARGE CAPS for all speakers-from-beyond), it's possible for the reader to skip along the upper-case dictation and jump over the less electrifying lower-case passages, which serve largely as connective matter, and are spoken in the author's own rather chatty voice.

Such skipping is not only possible, in fact, but at times necessary, for Merrill's "net of loose talk tightening to verse"—the narrative couplets with which he stitches together his verse novel—is knit too slackly. The weak patches tend to multiply, with the speed of composition, halfway into "Mirabell"; whereupon there develops too much nattering in couplets between Merrill and dead friends we didn't know, too much gossip about the globe-trotting of the author and his fellow medium, David Jackson ("I thanked my stars / When I lost the Leica at Longchamps"). The first unsettling visitations of the super-angels make good dramatic poetry but their later appearances seem too predictable and formalized, video cassettes programmed to fill up the time between jets to Greece or the Orient.

Still, when future archeologists of literature come to poke over the bones of this century's poetry, James Merrill's strange, long works using the ouija board will at the very least give pause, like a mastodon with wings.

Shimmering Nets

In this small book of poems (Kit Robinson's fourth), "meaning" in the traditional sense is something that on first inspection seems to come through only in occasional hints and snatches (a line mentioning the Bayshore Freeway, or another alluding to musician Charley [Bird] Parker). It creates transitory referential moments in what is otherwise a purely verbal landscape.

In normal discourse, the flow of sense can be pursued continuously from one word and phrase to the next, much as in the Burma-Shave signs that used to line our highways.

Here, however, it's as if the "signs" were blank, a series of empty billboards (non sequiturs), whose only sense is discontinuous; all continuity must be supplied by the reader, who quickly comes to feel like someone traveling unfamiliar terrain in the dark with no batteries in his flashlight.

There's more to this, though, than just an obstinate desire to be difficult. Kit Robinson *is* difficult, but in a way that's quite intriguing; difficulty for its own sake is boring, one thing *Riddle Road* is not.

The most elegant and accomplished specimen of Robinson's intriguing technique is "In the Orpheum Building," a poem written entirely in abruptly amputated lines. Its incomplete sentences hang in space, like cliffs, Piranesi-esque bridges to nowhere. In sequence, such lines occasion a haunting sense of discontinuity that constantly flirts with discursive statement, but never really attains it. ("Single story two bed-

---

Review of *Riddle Road* by Kit Robinson, *San Francisco Chronicle*, 1983.

room dwelling across from / Parts unknown and won't be back and hesitates / To hand over that strongbox. . . . ")

By building up an anticipatory expectation of meaning, then stubbornly postponing its fulfillment, Robinson playfully manipulates the reader's involvement. Left hanging by his unfinished lines, our urge is to complete them for him, to meld non sequitur into non sequitur, creating a new kind of sense. On our own, we make up an atmosphere of meaning to fill the vacuum in which the poet has abandoned us.

It's an invention he encourages by offering us, here and there in the poem, certain key lines that seem to carry a dominant weight—signposts looming out of the fog to tell us where we are. Such naturalistic fragments give us the reassuring feeling that the poem is finally coming into focus:

> with a background of factory stacks. Hopper's city,
> because the walls are brick and in the sun, so bright
> ("In the Orpheum Building")

These lines, along with the poem's title, are clues that allow us—like archeologists hesitantly rebuilding a ruined city according to recovered fragments of its original architectural plan—to begin reconstructing the poem's absent "sense." With the fragmentary suggestion of an Edward Hopper cityscape as guide, other allusive details seem to lock into place, and the puzzling impenetrability of "In the Orpheum Building" breaks down as imagination comes into focus.

The quality of the poem lies in its ability to lead us through several such tentative approaches to comprehension, only to deny us persistently the comfortable certainty that we're on the right track. It's a poem of open-ended discovery, and as such remains both maddening and remarkably pleasing (for its teasing of the imagination is as pleasurable as it is elusive).

The mysterious final line of another poem, "Tree Vagrancy"—"I find in the world"—works as a sort of internal revelation of Robinson's procedure in this book. Robinson "finds in the world" a brilliant conundrum, a riddle as intricate as the shimmering nets of suggestion that connect words and things.

The Nouveau Abstraction

In the pool hall of contemporary poetry—especially in the Bay Area, where the sheer number of players always makes the level of competition appear deceptively elevated—a style I like to call the nouveau abstraction currently rules the table.

"My subject is language," proclaims poet Stephen Rodefer, in one stroke both defining and aligning himself with the nouveau abstraction. A poetic movement that voluntarily carries a heavy dragweight of opacity, it makes "non linear" word structures its point and largely rejects such time-honored ingredients as drama, tension, narrative, beginning, middle, end.

To give the nouveau abstraction its due, it's certainly serious. (In fact, it packs a mighty wallop of Catch-22 type aesthetic strategizing.) "It is to be noted that when any part of this paper appears dull," Richard Steele once joked in the *Tatler,* "there is a design in it." The nouveau abstraction says exactly the same thing, but it isn't joking.

Period styles come and go, but while they're around, they have the contextual effect of self-legitimization. Flat greyness appears to take on life and color when seen against a backdrop of more flat greyness; painters Rothko and Newman proved this phenomenon long ago. In a blank field, a single speck can look interesting, even "dynamic."

Like any period style, nouveau abstraction has its exceptional practitioners.

Gloria Frym might turn out to be the best of them. She

Review of *Back to Forth* by Gloria Frym and *Four Lectures* by Stephen Rodefer, *San Francisco Chronicle,* 1983.

endows each of her small self-contained word units with a spherical perfection—like a Calder mobile so exquisitely made it will rotate forever, sans apparent outside motive force.

"Underneath the skin of silence, the custard of words bubbles," Frym notes reflexively in *Back to Forth.* "There is much danger in protecting yourself with too many words . . . all words have a hidden future . . . all of your problems have to do with words."

Words are Frym's brilliant obsession. The neurotic intensity in her post-surrealist prose-poem line is both striking and compulsive, almost disqualifying her from the nouveau abstraction because it demonstrates a powerful hunger for feeling.

Frym's work reminds me most of the paintings and writings of Giorgio de Chirico (Frym probably gets her de Chiricoism via New York poet John Ashbery). It spins silently in a perfectly constructed, emotionally dilated, slightly menacing and certainly enigmatic space. It goes nowhere, but its presence deposits a small steady shadow on your imagination.

Back to Forth is co-winner of this year's San Francisco State University Poetry Center book award. The other honoree is Stephen Rodefer's *Four Lectures.* Both books are produced by The Figures, a press that actively promulgates the nouveau abstraction.

Rodefer, a Berkeley writer like Frym, is concerned with rescuing poetry from an "exhaustion of form" (Frym's term), which is really a task triply difficult: to truly know all the old forms are exhausted you must exhaust yourself in exhausting them, thus running the risk of leaving *yourself* too exhausted to continue. But Rodefer does persevere, with surprising persistence, not to mention an "eloquence" and "nobility" (to quote award judge Anselm Hollo) and "solidity" and "usefulness" (Robert Creeley) that have attracted notable poet-critics to this book.

It is "writing writing": nonstop, inclusive, full-on, nervy, loquacious ("Enjoy the heads of your beaches, I'm not going in order / to get tied up on spec, but I wanted to meet your fellow brains . . ."), but perhaps a little too accurately titled for my taste. I don't care much for lectures anyway, much less lectures on language, and I'm bored by "talk," especially in poetry.

Saying your subject is language is the same thing as saying you really don't have any subject, but want to say something nonetheless. You are, in the familiar expression, talking to hear yourself talk—risking the reaction the girl gets in the old Joe Jones tune, "You Talk Too Much."

There's a pure beauty in language, but there's also an arrogance in all formal resolutions ("the subject is language . . ."). That's probably the point of the parable of Noah's descendants, who for their presumption in trying to build the ultimate structural abstraction—a tower to reach to heaven—were cursed with having their words made unintelligible even to each other.

A Small Fist of Words

Robert Creeley's *Collected Poems,* comprising all his work published in books and magazines between 1945 and 1975, is the full, careful account of a very discriminating intelligence tracking itself—both as autobiography and as art. With this poet, the two things have always been inextricable. As he put it some thirty years ago, his "form" and his "content" are merely mutual extensions, neither capable of standing alone.

Creeley's best known contribution to contemporary poetics is that dictum, *Form is an extension of content,* which today rings like some casual conundrum unless one considers the context from which it comes. A comparatively underprivileged New England chicken farmer, Creeley came of age as a poet in the 1950s, a time when a sort of social hegemony had overcome literary values. The predominant poetic mode in this country was then the imitation of elaborate verse-forms taken from previous epochs: a whole generation of American poets—mostly comfortably ensconced in the groves of academe—made poems like ships in bottles; the degree of difficulty, not the music or truthfulness, seemed to be the main criterion of excellence. These poets adopted such time-tested formal vessels as the sestina, the villanelle, etc., and then poured into them sentiments which often bore only an arbitrary or accidental relation to the form. The result was the building of many baroque edifices of language, sometimes admirably crafted, sometimes ludicrous, but rarely expressive of deep or direct feeling.

Review of *The Collected Poems of Robert Creeley: 1945–1975,* San Francisco Chronicle, 1983.

By suggesting that, conversely, the form of a poem be developed spontaneously or "organically" out of the urgency of the message it contains—with feeling, but without contrivance—Creeley was proposing a whole new set of priorities. Direct speech, itself a formal act, was now to be presented in its original, stripped-down condition, rather than inverted or inflected to drape over a structure induced from outside.

The radical effects of Creeley's proposition can't be underestimated. Its first (and still best) examples were his own early lyrics, now collected here *in toto*. Each was, indeed (as the poet has said), a highly "compressed statement—even the spacing of lines shrunk to a small fist of words, defensive and altogether by itself." As tautly complex as strong emotion, yet as delicately musical as the songs of Thomas Campion (one of Creeley's major influences), these short poems were primarily innovative in their reductiveness and essentialism: only the absolutely necessary words were there; and there were rarely more than a few of them.

The upshot, historically, was an immediate demystification of the poem. No longer was it crucial (or even sensible) to invite your soul in fancy Augustan stanza forms or record your domestic life in shapes taken from classic odes. This opened up poetry to thousands of writers who'd been intimidated by a decade of poems that had simply looked too much like Grecian urns to be *true*. After Creeley, came a deluge of new, modest bards, very few with anything like his Puritan severity of mind or Elizabethan soundness of ear, but all working the same territory, creating a mass-democratic cottage verse that ushered postwar American poetry outside the halls of fading ivy, and in turn made possible a whole new generation of "post modern" academicism (not Creeley's fault, but isn't it always the way?).

What's ironic about this is that Creeley, for all his inventiveness, shows himself in the copious new *Collected Poems* (and in several recent chapbooks not included here) to be a sort of traditionalist *manqué*. Taken together, his poems reflect the obvious modernist influences—D. H. Lawrence, W. C. Williams, Ezra Pound. But even more powerfully, they echo, and extend, a pure, compressed English lyric line: from the intense, yet desperately "courtly" obsession of the lover, as in Wyatt or Campion, to the elegiac, nostalgic quality, or the sober, wry realism, as in Thomas Hardy, their range is described by the past. Not bound by it, but not fully comprehensible without it.

Movements in literature come and go, even the most passionate of them. "Time passes / love in the dark." But this poet's achievement stands clear in the daylight, now, and will last.

Lives of the Poets

England is as justly famous for its bards as for tea, royalty and cricket. John Milton, Robert Browning and W. H. Auden are among the most prominent of them. Each has been memorialized in Westminster Abbey and held up for study in schools on both sides of the Atlantic. A major by-product of their prominence has been an immense body of published comment on their works and lives.

That corpus weighs heavy on the backs of contemporary critics and biographers as they struggle to make some fresh contribution. The few original masterpieces of recent "classic" literary biography—for example, Walter J. Bate's great books on Johnson, Keats and Coleridge—are outnumbered by myopic scholarly exhumations and lame "pop" re-hashes.

What, then, of these latest entries? A. N. Wilson, a respected English novelist and literary editor of the *Spectator,* has written a novelistic and argumentative account of Milton's life that proposes new slants—sometimes piquant, more often gratuitously speculative—on old facts.

Wilson's scholarly virtuosity and love of learning resembles Milton's own in at least one dimension, that of the pride he takes in flaunting it; his book becomes a kind of hobbyhorse heaven. His pet theory, involving the significance of Milton's interest in Italian music, gets ridden harder than a six-year-old plug in a claiming race.

Review of *The Life of John Milton* by A. N. Wilson, *Robert Browning: A Life Within Life* by Donald Thomas, and *Auden: A Carnival of Intellect* by Edward Callan, *San Francisco Chronicle,* 1983.

It is inevitable that one who writes a life of Milton must run into the problem of the great poet's insufferable personality. Wilson's answer to this—to proclaim, defend and justify—drives him into some difficult corners when it comes to interpreting the poet's life. He was "arrogant, lofty, snobbish and cruel," this Milton of Wilson's—yet when the poet's young wife leaves him after only a few weeks of marriage, Wilson peremptorily dismisses her mother's report that the break was owed to Milton's nature and goes on to give his own opinion: that, though Milton was a perfectly acceptable husband, his wife was "kidnaped" by "possessive relations."

In discussing Milton's poetry, Wilson is best on *Paradise Lost,* that sublime and lofty poem which later caused Joseph Addison to quip, "our language sunk under him." In a sense unintended by Addison, Milton's very grandness did bog the language down. The poet of *Paradise Lost* had twisted the mother tongue into the mold of languages he preferred, Latin and Italian. Two hundred years later, the inversions and circumlocutions of his style still clung to the Victorian verse.

Among its victims was the youthful Robert Browning, whose long "Miltonesque" poem *Sordello* was such a tortuous disaster that Thomas Carlyle, a Browning supporter, claimed his wife "had read the six books of the poem and was none the wiser as to whether Sordello was a man, a town, or a book."

As Donald Thomas shows in his biography, Browning's principal achievement as a poet, and his principal legacy to the future of English poetry, was to turn away from the style of *Sordello* toward a psychological realism and conversational tone distinctly "modern," which strongly influenced certain twentieth-century writers—including Auden, whose "Musée des Beaux Arts" makes direct use of one of Browning's casual, occasional narratives.

Thomas, who has also written books about Swinburne and the Marquis de Sade, portrays Browning as modern in ways that went beyond mere verse style. His Browning is a turbulent, morbid and obsessed figure who nonetheless "maintains" admirably in marriage and career, eventually (and ironically) winning acclaim for the more hygienic moments ("O to be in England / Now that April's there") in an oeuvre studded with narratives of life in the ethical lower depths. As Thomas points out, even Browning's "God's in his heaven, All's right with the world" comes from a poem ("Pippa Passes") that's actually about murder, adultery and prostitution.

Browning's natural morbidity, Thomas suggests, leaked out only in his poetry, which was expressive of his true psychological makeup. Lionized by polite society, Thomas's Browning lived in his poetry a secret "life within life." The term is from Alfred Adler, and Thomas's drift—making of the private, poetic Browning a "darkside" figure who suffered through his special romantic agonies in his verse—tempts us to expect a full airing of the psychology of this archetypal Victorian writer. We don't get that. Instead we get a fairly competent conventional biography, with the "darkside" Browning emerging only in moments of sad bathos, as when, while supposedly mourning his recently deceased wife, Elizabeth Barrett, he writes some dirty letters to another woman.

Like Milton, who in his early twenties vowed to "obtain immortal fame" through poetry, W. H. Auden was convinced of his vocation at an early age—determining to become "a great poet" even during his university days at Oxford. And Auden, too, went on to make verse that fulfilled these high aspirations, "expressing the age" in which he lived. It is this quality of Auden's work that Edward Callan, a scholar and critic from Western Michigan University, chooses to focus on.

The drama of Auden's career, as Callan views it, resides in his development from an early sense of the poet as social and political propagandist to a later conviction that poetry is, or should be, essentially disengaged from action—a medium which "makes nothing happen."

The turning point in this conversion, Callan suggests, came around 1938, when Auden rejected the intuitive, romantic bias of one of his early heroes, the Irish poet W. B. Yeats—a bias, Auden suspected, which would inevitably lead to self-deception, self-indulgence and even totalitarianism. Auden's reaffirmation of Christianity around this same time, Callan tells us, resulted as much from the intellectual reaction against Yeats and romanticism as from a serious emotional rebuff inflicted by his lover, Chester Kallman.

It is crucial to Callan's method, indeed, that we accept the paramount importance of ideas in determining the course of the poet's behavior. Auden is here viewed as the quintessential modern intellectual—well-read, widely informed, self-conscious, constantly "responding imaginatively" to the "Weltanschauung of [his] times"—hence the presence in so many Auden poems of the ideas of Freud, Marx, Kierkegaard, Tillich and other "modern thinkers." If poetry "made nothing happen," as Auden came to believe, his own nonetheless mirrored quite accurately the intellectual climate of the time in which it came into being.

That point is made at length, in detail, and with a dryness that occasionally evokes the stale air of libraries, in Callan's useful but rather slow-moving "intellectual biography."

Sleep before Evening

John Ashbery's new volume of poems is grounded in the mysterious seriousness and existential banality of daily experience, the ominous contingency and giddy confusion of human events, the fugitive clarities of perception and feeling that uplift us and impel us onward toward the ultimate truth of life.

These are the time-honored subjects of philosophical poetry, and that is what Ashbery is writing here, even when he employs the mode and format of the lyric—as in "At North Farm," one of the finest short poems in recent memory. It begins:

> Somewhere someone is traveling furiously toward you,
> At incredible speed, traveling day and night
> Through blizzard and desert heat, across torrents, through
>   narrow passes.
> But will he know where to find you, Recognize you when he
>   sees you,
> Give you the thing he has for you?

The menacing gift to be proffered by this dogged pursuer is the same one each of us can expect to receive from fate at the end of our days. But when will that end come, and will we be forewarned, and ready to receive it when it arrives? Those questions hang in the air over all the best poems in this book, creating its central drama.

It is the same drama that has affected poets' imaginations

Review of *A Wave* by John Ashbery, *San Francisco Chronicle,* 1984.

perennially—"When I have fears that I may cease to be . . ." Ashbery, at the apogee of a poetic career now acknowledged by even those tardy judges—the academic critics—to be a brilliant one, pauses as Keats once did to glance up over his shoulder toward the heavens, reading there a destiny which may choose to terminate his oeuvre at any moment. ("I think a lot about it," he writes in one poem, "The omnipresent possibility of being interrupted / While what I stand for is still almost a bare canvas.")

To pay attention to the business of living, toying with a rich present in "this plush solitude" of modern life, is a way of placating that avenging angel who is always "traveling furiously toward you" with his dark gift. Avoiding the knowledge of death is a form of denial necessary for daily existence. But, the poet seems to ask here, isn't this everyday sense of security a false one? "Is it enough / That the dish of milk is set out at night, / That we think of him sometimes, / Sometimes and always, with mixed feelings?"

Such questions are addressed throughout Ashbery's book, but with greatest articulation in the two works that frame it, the introductory "At North Farm" and the concluding set piece "A Wave," a dense, 700-line meditative excursus which stands with the earlier *Three Poems* and *Self-Portrait in a Convex Mirror* as one of the poet's most powerful extended productions.

"A Wave" deepens the book's primary proposal, that there exists a complex and ironic bond between unconsciousness and death—the former serving at times as a pleasant escape from the latter, even while imitating it and hastening its arrival. "To pass through pain and not know it, / A car door slamming in the night" are the poem's opening lines. Relaxation of perception is freedom from pain. But, we hear a few pages later: "We will all have to walk back this way / A second time, and not to know it then, not / To number each straggling piece of sagebrush / Is to sleep before evening."

"To sleep before evening" is to step out of the picture before its outlines are complete—something an artist as thorough and deliberate as Ashbery (or any serious poet) dreads to do. And yet acceptance of the gravity of fate is at the heart of human understanding, whether that of the artist or of the ordinary human being (for every artist is also that). "A Wave" builds to this acceptance, this

> . . . cimmerian moment, in which all lives, all destinies
> And incompleted destinies were swamped
> As though by a giant wave that picks itself up
> Out of a calm sea and retreats again into nowhere
> Once its damage is done

Enigmatic Arguments

"One must be absolutely modern." French poet Arthur Rimbaud's concise dictum at once created and defined modernist poetry a century ago; poetry since then has been preoccupied with living up to it. This modernist century's ultimate poet, perhaps, is John Ashbery, whose work has managed to keep a step ahead of successive waves of the avant-garde for some three and a half decades, constantly assimilating and anticipating newness in a manner responsive to Rimbaud's dictum.

The 138 poems here are selected by the poet from his ten collections, including *Some Trees* (1956), *The Tennis Court Oath* (1962), *The Double Dream of Spring* (1970), *Self-Portrait in a Convex Mirror* (1975) and *A Wave* (1984). They range in length from haiku and short lyrics to long prose poems ("The System," from *Three Poems*) and major long poems in verse, like the title pieces from *Self-Portrait in a Convex Mirror* and *A Wave.*

Seen in this chronological order, the curve of Ashbery's development is clear—from the playful, discreet aestheticism of *Some Trees* through the rigorous mystery and enigma of the *Tennis Court* period (less well-represented here than one might wish) to the ominous, brooding, philosophic fatality of the poems from *A Wave*, with their overriding image of death arriving like some avenging angel.

Ashbery was one of the first poets to not only accept, tolerate and admit freely into his work the quality of mystery or enigma created by ambiguity, but also deliberately cultivate it.

Review of *Selected Poems* by John Ashbery, *Los Angeles Herald Examiner*, 1986.

The surprise elements in his poetry, its unexpected "chance" twists of thought and syntax, its unpredictable shifts of tone and address are more than the mere "surrealistic tomfoolery" they've been called. Such elements play as productive a role in Ashbery's writing as they do in action painting (Pollock) or aleatory music (Stockhausen), hinting in all three places of the complex relations that exist between imagination and the halo of indeterminacy surrounding it.

Ashbery has often used musical analogies to describe his poetry. What he likes about music, he has said, is "its ability of being convincing, of carrying an argument through successfully to the finish, though the terms of this argument remain unknown quantities."

The key word there is "unknown." "The poet must make himself a seer," Rimbaud said, "for he arrives at the unknown." The terms of Ashbery's arguments are as evasive and enigmatic as their syntax. Like a dissonant music that seems unfamiliar until recognized in the beguiling moment of its disappearance, these arguments make sense not rationally but emotionally, as they continually escape us.

One Big Movie

"It's all blended into one big movie." That comment of John Lennon's, looking back shortly before his death at the wild landscape of his life in the 1960s, might also be applied to this huge autobiographical primer.

Allen Ginsberg's position as a poet is in many ways similar to the one Lennon held as a musician, that of an accomplished artist whose extracurricular power as a cultural spokesman has given his work a range of effect rivaling that of popular political or religious leaders. The exceptional thing about Ginsberg's achievement of such wide social influence is the unusual medium he employed to attain it. Even if poets have always been, as Shelley suggested, society's unacknowledged legislators, Ginsberg has gone one step further, attempting not only to edify and enlighten through his verse, but also to create social change through his non-poetic activity—teaching, touring, proselytizing, conducting a nonstop, self-consuming crusade on behalf of kindness, compassion and mellow understanding in human affairs.

To attain the distinguished status of statesman, of course, any artist risks the loss of personal privacy routinely. Allen Ginsberg, it must be said, seems even to woo this loss. Self-exposure has always been his stock-in-trade as an artist. In fact it's also been his principal poetic innovation, extending to new lengths the large-scale autobiographical expansiveness of Walt Whitman. Whitman's vow to go "undisguised and naked" in his poetry echoes as a mere hollow threat compared to

---

Review of *Collected Poems: 1947–1980* by Allen Ginsberg, *San Francisco Chronicle,* 1984.

the actions of Ginsberg, who's never hesitated to take off his clothes in his poetry. Among those influenced by this, incidentally, was Lennon; would the leader of the world's most popular musical group have consented to appear in the nude on a national magazine cover if he hadn't known Allen Ginsberg?

Indeed, in poetry, self-exposure and success have been inclined to walk hand in hand for some time now. When you list the most popular poets of the last two-and-a-half decades—Robert Lowell among academics, Sylvia Plath among women, Allen Ginsberg with everybody else—you're looking at a lineup of publicly displayed compulsions and obsessions that would in previous times have been considered material for a psychotherapist, not a critic.

Ginsberg, of course, reveals more of himself than anybody, and with less evidence of guilt or embarrassment en route. His candor is so legendary that it's almost consoling to know there's at least one poem he's kept in the closet all these years for reasons of "prudence"—a frank narrative of his first sexual encounter with Neal Cassady. It's here. Also included are all the rest of Ginsberg's sexual and psychic skeletons: passages once seen as flagrant, now familiar, even user-friendly.

Whether you think of all this reckless revelation as exhibitionism or honesty (perhaps there's at least a little of each in it), it has helped make Ginsberg the truly "global" poet he always intended to be. In the past twenty-five years he's bared his soul from whistle-stop to whistle-stop, everywhere poetry can be transported, disseminating along the way a personal program of world salvation—differing slightly in content from era to era, as love, marijuana and flowers gave way to antiwar and antiheroin, and then in turn to meditation, deep breathing and neo-Tibetan obeisance.

If there were elections for the office of World Poet, Ginsberg would certainly be the odds-on favorite. For despite his education in the craft from such "purist" masters as Kerouac, Apollinaire, Pound and William Carlos Williams, his real affinity as a writer is with the other World Poets—his predecessors and fellows, from Blake and Whitman to Neruda and Yevtushenko. What's a World Poet? Well, when Ginsberg visited recently to read at the UC-Berkeley campus a few blocks from the Milvia Street cottage where he'd once (1955) toiled as an obscure young poet, producing "Sunflower Sutra" and "A Supermarket in California," tickets were scarce, and the demand for interviews so intense that a five-minute press conference had to be organized after the reading. A few days later he left for China; by the time you read this, he might be in San Salvador, Tel Aviv or Havana. Where history goes, Allen Ginsberg's never far behind—once on buses, nowadays usually on 747s.

It's no shock, then, that Ginsberg often slips into mistaking his own personal journey for the spiritual life of his time. The poems are a record of it all, now truly and finally blended, to hark back to Lennon's term, into "one big movie." With the poems here placed for the first time in the original order of their composition, the *Collected* is no less than the story of Allen Ginsberg's life: "the actual movie of my mind," as he once called his poetry, now extended from a series of short features into a single vast self-chronicle-cum-historical opus, "Song of Myself" meets *Birth of a Nation*.

And if Ginsberg is—as critic Helen Vendler has called him—the self-appointed "biographer of his time," then he's also a biographer who's reading back the life to the subject constantly, in hopes of converting it to his own version of universal heart-to-heart tenderness.

The poems, unfortunately, have tended increasingly meanwhile to get obscured by the smoke and thunder of the media image, beginning with the storm over his first, censored major work, *Howl* (1956), and continuing through Ginsberg's subsequent good-natured and generous involvement in public life. He has been perceived variously as a dangerous lunatic with a messianic complex, or as a silly, well-meaning but "hairy loss" (Kerouac), or as a visionary prophet.

Yet very little serious, unbiased attention has been paid to his poetry, which has largely been regarded as somehow after the fact. The *Collected* both invites and makes possible such attention, because here at last the whole work can be seen intact, divided chronologically into ten sections representing respective phases of Ginsberg's career and travels—e.g., Section VII, "King of May: America to Europe (1963–1965)"—

and supported by a set of back-end "Notes" intended by the author to "transmit cultural archetypes to electronic laser TV generations that don't read Dostoevsky or Buddha bibles." (The "Notes" are in fact quite copious, comprising what Ginsberg with typically disarming twinkle calls "mini-essays" to "hint further reading for innocent-eyed youths.")

The poems themselves break down into two general types, differing significantly in approach and method; Ginsberg really uses two distinct styles. The first, or high style, is that of the Vatic Utterance, prophetic in intent, rhapsodic in tone, often ranting, incantatory or oracular in delivery, usually composed in long jazz-chorus-like lines, with great rhythmic insistence. Ginsberg has attributed this style frankly to Jack Kerouac, acknowledging that "the long saxophone-like chorus lines" of poems like *Howl* (which, not coincidentally, got its title from Kerouac) are direct, energetic descendants of the dense Kerouacian prose rush—"Kerouac invented and initiated my practice of speech-flow prosody," Ginsberg wrote in 1956. The methods of structuring his long-line poems, however, are often Ginsberg's own, usually employing syntactical repetition.

Along this "chain of strong-breath'd poems" can be found what Ginsberg in the preface to the *Collected* accurately calls his "peaks of inspiration"—*Howl, Kaddish*, etc. These are authentic major works. He has said elsewhere that such poems come from states of "prophetic illuminative seizure." One is tempted to suspect, however, that long practice and study in writing had at least as much to do with it.

It should also be said that among the later of these rhapsodic, long-line poems can be found some of Ginsberg's more embarrassing moments, such as the oozing servitude and masochistic groveling of "Please Master" (1968), that tests the limits of the confessional mode to extreme degree ("Please master call me a dog, an assbeast . . . please master order me down on the floor," etc.).

A second style can be found in the poems that populate what Ginsberg describes as his "valleys"—i.e., his occasional verses, comprising the personal documentary of experience that makes up the bulk of this book. Most of them are simply diaristic notations. The associative, short-circuit logic of his notational images—"hydrogen jukebox," "locomotive river-bank," etc.—is something Ginsberg claims to have borrowed from Kerouac's "sketching" method and from the paintings of Cézanne, but with time he's evolved it into something as distinctly his own as the cracked rabbinical moan of his public reading style.

Ginsberg divides the occasional poems from his rhapsodic works categorically, even dismissing them in one comment as "just diddling away"—and indeed, their miscellaneous, un-sorted quality makes it hard not to regard the general run of them as just that. While there are many excellent occasional poems here, it remains true that the unedited "actual movie" of Ginsberg's mind is sometimes less than gripping, such as when he's bumping along on endless buses and trains through Kansas or India. This is the poet, of course, who once re-ported without irony in a poem that "I took a crap once this day—How extraordinary it all goes!" Too often, the diary-style poems degenerate into mere lists of experiential trivia, captured in all their "suchness" with self-effacing honesty, but not organized in any compelling way.

In many respects Ginsberg's entire poetic approach is sur-prisingly modest; he imposes few judgments on his experi-ence, and rarely employs syntax to distribute his juxtaposed images into cause-and-effect structures, preferring instead the freshness and immediacy of the untampered flow of the "movie" of impressions through the mind. This is an intuitive, emotional, physically responsive approach, one which trans-fers lists of images and feelings with great clarity, but rarely arrives at a form beyond the personal/autobiographical.

This said, it's clear that some of the nearly 900 pages of poetry in this book could have been left out, if aesthetics alone were the editorial measure. But by throwing it all into the cinematic blender, Ginsberg has concocted a fascinating, com-pulsively revealing montage-style autobiography that also con-stitutes a "biography of our time." OK, America, this is your life—or anyway one man's movie of it.

More Big Movie

The poems in *White Shroud* were composed on a jetliner high above the American plains; on a bus in Mexico; in New York and Boulder; in Managua, Baoding and Shanghai. If Allen Ginsberg isn't the world's first truly international poet, he'll do until one comes along.

A missionary of peace and meditation, Ginsberg in China finds himself caught up in "ignorant and contentious" throes of self. ("I spent lunch / arguing about boys making love with a student.") When a persistent cough sends him to his hotel room bed, "reclusive . . . a sick guest in a vast poor kingdom," he reflects unhappily on his so-so performance as a cultural ambassador: "I'm famous, / my poems have done some men good / and a few women ill, perhaps the good / outweighs the bad, I'll never know. / Still I feel guilty I haven't done more" ("Reading Bai Juyi"). For Ginsberg, the China trip triggers self-revelation; but then, with this poet, *everything* does.

But Ginsberg's song of himself has become an increasingly discordant one over the years. His free-associating list poems remain Whitmanesque in their sheer cataloging energy. But what's cataloged is mostly signs of physical decay, the griefs and woes of aging. Some of these pages carry the ring of clinical records, like the kvetching of matrons at a health farm: "I've a pain in my back / Fifth lumbar & sacrum / Kidneystones alas alack . . . should lose ten pounds . . . Back pain a little, turn my head neck hurts . . . Right cheek paralyzed slightly, eye squints tired . . . Bald and panicky, with Pyronie's disease."

Review of *White Shroud: Poems 1980–1985* by Allen Ginsberg, *San Francisco Chronicle*, 1986.

The inventory of maladies and symptoms runs on: ear-itches, hair loss, sore gums, chronic hepatitis, smoker's cough, bronchitis, high blood pressure, Bell's palsy. We get a guided tour of the poet's medicine cabinet ("B complex bottled . . . nightly Clonadine Hydrochloric pills, athlete's foot Tolnaftate cream"), and even find out that his blood pressure pills "cause impotency!"

Under the self-imposed stress of having to save the globe even as he trots over it, Ginsberg asks himself questions at every stop. "Am I holding the world up right? . . . do I have enough $ to leave the rent paid while I'm in China?" "Hideous Public Karma" weighs him down; he feels "Telephones tingling down my spine." ("Nothing but thoughts, how solve World Problems by worrying in my bedroom?")

The funniest poem in this book—which has a number of good comic moments—turns his public-figureitis inside out, making appealing comedy of neurotic self-revelation: "Who is this Slave Master makes / me answer letters in his name / Write poetry year after year, keep up / appearances / Who is this egotist whose file cabinets / leave no room for more / pictures of Me?" ("I'm a Prisoner of Allen Ginsberg"). Distressed by his own "public sound, bank accounts, Master Charge," Ginsberg finds that life at sixty contains an equal mixture of vestigial desire ("I needed a young musician take off his pants sit down on the bed & sing the blues") and the wisdom of renunciation: "I've got to give up / Books, checks, letters / File cabinets, apartment / pillows, bodies and skin / even the ache in my teeth" ("It's All So Brief").

The book's weakest links are the political pieces, primarily the songs (for some of which, musical notation has been included). Granted these might come off better when sung (and given Ginsberg's voice, the "might" gets the emphasis there), it's hard to defend the way they look in the cold black and white of print. They tend to doggerel, express displeasure about such things as the "New Right," "National Police," "Big Business," "Exxon," "Mobil," "Network News," "KKK," etc., and contain lines like these (in a song about U.S. involvement in Nicaragua): "Make a tomb / for men & boys / ending joy / of villages / and pillage / or burn down / to the ground / little huts

/ where pigs rut / This costs much / tax money as such / for an error / or red terror . . ." ("The Little Fish Devours the Big Fish").

But to leap from bathos to sublimity in the turning of a page is an old Ginsberg trick. Never has that leap been longer than it is here, from the low moments of the songs to the high point of this book, the title poem "White Shroud."

In some senses this piece closes a circle for Ginsberg, returning to the theme and style of his early masterpiece "Kaddish," but with a difference. As then, the poem's key figure is the poet's dead mother, but the prevailing tone is no longer one of pain and loss but of redemption and reconciliation—an understanding of death that renews life. And, though it echoes the long dense lines of the earlier poem, this time the "breath" rhythms seem less nervous and eccentric, more settled, almost classical in their limber narrative cadence.

After a brief rhymed introduction à la Blake ("I am summoned from my bed / To the Great City of the Dead / Where I have no house or home / But in dreams may sometime roam / Looking for my ancient room"), Ginsberg launches into long, periodic lines: "I found myself in the Great Eastern Metropolis, / wandering under Elevated Transport's iron struts . . ." Like Dante, who in the middle of his life found himself in a dark wood, Ginsberg begins his poem by letting us know it's to be a quest from dark to light, or lost to found.

Having returned in his dreams to "North Manhattan," seeking a home, he wanders "tenement embankments" in "West Bronx / looking for my own hot-water furnished flat to settle in . . . anxious I be settled with money in my own place before / nightfall." The dream-streets he travels first resemble "Paris or Budapest suburbs," then become a "picture cavalcade" of New York images c. 1935, a "newspaper metropolis" that wells up from "bookshelf decades ago":

> double-decker buses in September sun near Broadway El,
> skyscraper roofs upreared ten thousand office windows
>   shining
> electric-lit above tiny taxis street lamp'd in Mid-town
> avenues' late-afternoon darkness the day before Christmas,

Herald Square crowds thronged past traffic lights July noon
    to lunch
Shop under Macy's department store awnings for dry goods
pause with satchels at Frankfurter counters wearing stylish
    straw
hats of the decade, mankind thriving in their solitudes in
    shoes.

Through this busy dream-jungle of images the questing poet moves, meeting up with ghosts; first his Russian Jewish grandmother (who "lay in her bed and sighed eating a little Chicken / soup"), and then, in a "side alley on a mattress," an aged, toothless "shopping-bag lady" with "cranky hair, half paralyzed, complaining angry"—his mother, Naomi, "older than I knew her before / her life disappeared." The discovery terminates the dreamer's wanderings, "those years unsettled . . . over now." He decides to move in with Naomi, sharing a "mortal life" in "her cave," an "unpainted storeroom," where he will "cook and write books for a living."

This passage, proceeding from the intense emotion of the reunion ("Here I could live / forever, here have a home, with Naomi, at long last / at long last, my search was ended . . .") to the vintage Ginsbergian self-deflating humor of his domestic arrangements (he and his mother will even be able to "afford a telephone . . . call up Aunt Edie in California") is both a culmination of the poem's quest and a moving image of reconciliation that solves the poet's anxious questionings in this book. "My breast rejoiced," he declares, "What long-sought peace!" From that rhapsodic moment the poem tapers into its coda, wherein the dreamer awakens before dawn in his Boulder home, and descends, "glad of life," to begin a new day.

This memorable poem has a way of bathing the rest of Ginsberg's new work in its calm light, to some extent relieving the black-and-white, stenciled-in spareness of "political" vision in many of the surrounding pieces. "White Shroud," the poem, participates in politics even though it's apolitical. Like all authentic art, what it does is resist death—the ultimate domination—by allying itself with "our mortal life" so strongly.

A Bop Colorist

Twenty-five years ago Fred McDarrah, the *Village Voice* photographer, put together a book of his photos of the Greenwich Village hipster-Bohemian society of the 1950s. McDarrah called his work *The Beat Scene.* The photographs document a social epoch—skinny, unsmiling guys in beards and shades and sandals, serious-looking pony-tailed girls in tight slacks and turtlenecks, gathered together in coffeehouses or in cold water flats with tacky mattresses on the floor.

The featured subjects in McDarrah's book are some seventy-five "Beat" authors—Kerouac, Ginsberg, Ferlinghetti and many, many more who are now all but forgotten. One of the latter is poet-musician Howard Hart, a slender young fellow in dark glasses who, in McDarrah's book, stands next to a caged parrot and casts a sidelong glance across the page at one of his poems.

Fame may have passed Howard Hart by for the past two-and-a-half decades, but now he's back—not as a historical footnote but as a writer to be reckoned with. It turns out he's been making poems all along, and the best of them are gathered in this very impressive volume.

Hart went to New York from Ohio in 1946, at the age of nineteen, and began studying musical composition, theory and counterpoint with classical composer Charles Mills. Six years later he met and befriended the great jazz drummer Kenny Clarke who, along with Charlie Parker, Thelonius Monk and Dizzy Gillespie, had been in on the birth of bebop

---

Review of *Selected Poems: Six Sets, 1951–1983* by Howard Hart, *San Francisco Chronicle,* 1984.

39

at Minton's Playhouse in Harlem in 1941. Mills, Clarke and another great jazz percussionist, Elvin Jones, were all powerful influences on Hart's work—not only his music, but his poetry, one of whose principal virtues is its distinction as sound and rhythm.

Howard Hart's own writing possesses the quality he attributes, in one poem, to Ravel: "a refinement of lyricism . . . bequeathed to you from Chopin, perhaps, or Haydn." In Hart's case, the bequest evidently comes from the whole history of modern music, beginning with Mozart, descending down to bop and beyond, as well as from the "tunes" of his fellow poets—foremost among them the American surrealist Philip Lamantia and that master of "spontaneous bop prosody," Jack Kerouac himself. (Hart, Lamantia, Kerouac and musician David Amram put on New York's first jazz-poetry shows in 1957–58.)

Many of Hart's best poems, indeed, seem to move like slow ballads played by an expert improvisatory jazz soloist: They establish a melody, linger to savor it, embellish it, vary on it, gradually build a whole new melody, and then end in an unpredictable flourish akin to a bop tag.

If the music of Hart's poems sometimes recalls Kerouac's *Mexico City Blues*, their wild range of sensory imagery often evokes the early surrealist work (*Ekstasis*, etc.) of Lamantia. Just as Hart contributes his own intricate time sense and gifts of ear, however, he also introduces polychromatic tonalities of image that are absolutely singular.

The choice of a vivid Tom Wesselman work for the full-color cover of *Selected Poems* is apt. Painterly color plays a central role in Hart's poems, serving as an intuitive emotional code à la Rimbaud. The poems also use color as a kind of para-logic, moving along on hinges of "black lacquer joined (to) peach," "blue trees," "pink fields," "black pearls," "an arc of sand coated with emeralds," "a sky of orange whispers." Hart's poetry does more than build a "fandango of images" (as he calls it), though; just consider the compressed expressive quality of a line like "the gray royalty in poor people's eyes."

All of Hart's abilities as musician and colorist-in-language are apparent in his poem, "Billie Holiday Four," which begins, "I speak of a purple lady" and slides with strange subtlety through "Beethoven" and "innocence" to a moving statement that somehow ties in death, Freud and refrigerators:

> Actually Freud and she could have created a masterpiece
> Of lyrical gray and blue case history
> But beige by Lady's skin pearls on mistletoe
> Didn't work at all
> Lady sang from the slow cavern of human grief
> I hate refrigerators.

Howard Hart left the Village in the sixties, traveled around the world, worked as a musician and translator, settled in Northern California in the seventies, and now lives and writes in San Francisco, where at the age of fifty-seven he's finally being published in the style he's long deserved.

Love, Death and the Muses

Robert Duncan is the East Bay's principal contribution to American poetry. His major works include *The Opening of the Field* (1960), *Roots and Branches* (1964) and *Bending the Bow* (1968). Since the last-named of those, Duncan has observed an intentional period of non-publication, a sort of literary vow of silence. Bringing us up to date with Duncan's writing of the last fifteen years, the new collection, *Ground Work: Before the War,* allows us to chart further developments in the work of this modern American master.

Duncan was born in Oakland in 1919, and after being raised in Central California by adoptive parents, returned to the university in Berkeley—attending that school from 1936 to 1938 and again, following a ten-year hiatus, from 1948 to 1950. The period of interruption in Duncan's formal education was a very eventful one for him, both personally and artistically: dropping out of school to pursue a love affair, he wound up on the East Coast, spent some time in the army (he received a psychiatric discharge in 1941), encountered New York City's literary underground, edited two magazines (the *Experimental Review* and *Phoenix*), and began to establish himself as a poet (his first book, *Heavenly City, Earthly City,* appeared in 1947).

Both his homoerotic sexual stance and his imaginative involvement with magic and romance—each of which was to impel strongly the direction of his later work—were devel-

Review of *Ground Work: Before the War* by Robert Duncan and *Young Robert Duncan: Portrait of the Poet as Homosexual in Society* by Ekbert Faas, *Oakland Tribune,* 1984.

oped during these years. On his return to the university in 1948 Duncan edited the *Berkeley Miscellany*. In later years, he was affiliated with the university library, helping to build its impressive collection of modern literature.

During the early stages of his career, Duncan found himself involuntarily engaged in breaking new ground for the public sexual expression of artists. His struggle to emerge as a writer while preserving his sexual integrity is the subject of a recent biography, *Young Robert Duncan* by Ekbert Faas.

Among the episodes recounted by Faas is the controversy involving Duncan and the powerful academic poet-critic John Crowe Ransom; Ransom, as editor of *The Kenyon Review*, rejected an already typeset Duncan poem, "An African Elegy," after learning of the publication of Duncan's essay, "The Homosexual in Society," a touchstone articulation of the gay writer's position in our culture. That such repressive action would be unlikely to occur today is largely the result of the perseverance of a few conscientious gay writers, with Duncan perhaps the most significant of them.

In the 1950s and 1960s Duncan's original and motivating poetic voice achieved for him a position of eminence in the literary life not only of the Bay Area but of the nation. His early poetry prepared the terrain for what was later known as the San Francisco Renaissance. His meeting in 1947 with the late Charles Olson, who at once termed Duncan "a beautiful poet," with "ancient, permanent wings of Eros—& of Orphism," led to Duncan's teaching stint under Olson at the historic Black Mountain College.

In the later 1950s Duncan worked through the Poetry Center in San Francisco to import many major writers for their first Bay Area public appearances. One of his peers, the poet Robert Creeley, has called Duncan "the poet of my generation who brought the communal world of this art forward again." And in speaking of Duncan's position on the literary scene, Creeley compares him with no lesser figures than Dante and Walt Whitman.

In his new book Duncan continues his long engagement with what he considers the primary realities of poetry: Love, Death and the difficult but joyful discipline of the Muses—

those deliverers of light and fire, music and dance in words. But there is now a new absorption in social and historical issues, apparent mainly in the ongoing poem-series, "Passages." These poems deal with the Vietnam War and its sociopolitical causes and context, confronting what Duncan terms "the mask of War and 'Development' behind which the industrial-military power complex hides a contempt and hatred for nature."

While such poems mark an important advance in Duncan's work, there are others that extend his sense of homage to the art in which he has labored so long—poems celebrating, echoing and amplifying the work of previous poets ranging from Dante, Pindar, Ben Jonson and Sir Walter Raleigh to Mallarmé, Wallace Stevens and Louis Zukofsky.

One surprising aspect of the text is its reproduction of Duncan's own typewritten manuscript pages, an unusual feature which might seem indulgent in a more conventional poet but with Duncan, whose long lines and irregular margins are particularly important to his purpose, adds some valuable insights into the nature of the work.

Robert Duncan currently lives in San Francisco and teaches at New College of California, where he continues his dedication to spreading the "little area of light" (as he expresses it in the new book) cast by the lamp of poetry. A recent serious illness—it's hoped his recovery will be speedy—has done much to remind local readers just how valuable a presence and resource Robert Duncan has been, for more years than some of his audience is even able to remember.

Soul Back Homeward

Ground Work II: In the Dark is all that one might have expected of Robert Duncan's last book, a work of grand depth and seriousness exploring the shadow lands between life and death and "before What Is . . . in the dark this state / that knows not sleep nor waking, nor dream / —an eternal arrest" ("After a Long Illness").

For this poet whose lyric voice was almost a match for the mythical Orpheus's in its capacity to coax harmonies out of wild contradictions, symbolic fulfillments seemed to flock like the birds charmed out of the trees in those Orphic myths. It's poetic justice, then, that his final book should appear within a few days of the dispersion of his mortal remains. After all, this was a poet who refused to believe in chance. "Creation," he said, "is everywhere intending." Obeying the "orders" of a cosmic creative intent constituted Duncan's life work. "The world floods the moment we write," he once said. "We don't get to sit down and push that world, or invent it."

Postmodernist social affiliations notwithstanding, his true poetic affinities were prior; talking just last year about his role in the Olson-Creeley push, he told me he'd always "lagged behind, consciously," feeling he "belonged to an older constellation."

That "older constellation" was the Orphic/Romantic, a tradition evolved out of medieval mystical hermeticism and neo-Platonism, and culminating in the nineteenth-century yearnings for transcendental wholeness—or what Duncan playfully

Review of *Ground Work II: In the Dark* by Robert Duncan, *Exquisite Corpse,* 1988.

called "altogetherness"—of those writers who were his real spiritual antecedents: Shelley, Blake, Nerval, Poe, Baudelaire, Whitman.

Duncan once defined the romantic as a condition in which the actual and the spiritual are revealed at the same time. ("Working in words I am an escapist," he said, "but I want every part of the actual world involved in my escape.") The title of his first book expressed this: *Heavenly City, Earthly City.* So does almost every poem here in his last one. As in so many earlier Duncan poems of sensuous erotic rapture, sexual communion yields ego-dissolving bliss in "an Eros/Amor/Love/Cycle": "O every thing / was in the passing away into the kiss." But much more prevalent as a subject here—"Now truly the sexual Eros will have / left me and gone his way"—is an equally paradox-embracing convergence of failing physical systems with psyche as death draws near "Secretly / in the dark."

Given the timing, it's indeed hard *not* to read this book as a journal of holy dying. Its very format is foretold in its eerie and stirring final lines, by an approaching shadow figure—no longer a desired lover but a "particular Death"—who dictates the disposition of the last two decades of the poet's work into two books, the 1983 *Ground Work I: Before the War,* and this one:

> "I have given you a cat in the dark," the voice said.
> Everything changed in what has always been there
> at work in the Ground: the two titles
> "Before the War," and now, "In the Dark"
>   underwrite the grand design.   The magic
>   has always been there,   the magnetic purr
>   run over me, the feel as of cat's fur . . .

The imminent arrival of the ending hanging over the story informs even the intimate pacing and measure of the verse here, weighing down the somber metric of a poem like "To Master Baudelaire": "When I come to Death's customs, / to the surrender of my nativities, / that office of the dark too I picture / as if there were a crossing over, / a going through a door."

To my ear the poem which accomplishes that measured "crossing-over" most dimensionally is "The Styx." Here the sacred mythic river of the Greeks—crossed by the souls of the dead on their journey from the realm of the living—becomes first a watercourse deep within the earth, then with typical Duncanesque doubleness a premonitory psychic dream-river, drawing the hesitant, divinely-originated soul back homeward.

> Styx　this carver of caverns beneath us is.
> Styx　this black water　this down-pouring.
> 　The well is deep . . .
> 　　The light of day is not as bright
> 　　as this crystal flowing . . .
>
> 　the river beneath the earth　we knew
> 　　we go back to.
> 　Styx pouring down in the spring from its glacial remove,
> 　　from the black ice.
>
> 　Fifty million years—from the beginning of what we are—
> 　　we knew the depth of this well to be.
>
> 　Fifty million years deep—but our knowing deepens
> 　　　　　—time deepens—
> 　　　　this still water
> 　we thirst for　in dreams we dread.

Even Orpheus's living song, which made actual rivers stand still, couldn't halt time's flow. Robert Duncan's poetry here completes its final paradox-resolving proposition, reminding us that the song itself becomes part of that great flow.

From Point A to Point X

In common with such fellow San Francisco poets as Robert Duncan and the late Jack Spicer, Kirby Doyle proposes total surrender to the art of poetry. ("I accept only th' teaching / of the poem.") All three belong in the poetic tradition of Inspiration/Imagination, which holds that poems are made of cosmic fire handed over from another dimension like a kind of Muses' Olympic torch. In this tradition, the "writer" is only a conductor, who gets his juice from elsewhere—somewhere outside his normal comprehension, conception or intention. This is a theory that goes back beyond the Greeks, and drifted down to the present by way of Blake, Shelley and the Surrealists, whose response was to invent "automatic writing"—as in Cocteau's *Orphée,* where the poet-hero gets his poems from radio broadcasts in a limousine supplied by the Underworld.

That Kirby Doyle belongs in this tradition is clear from "To Pat Friedman," a deceptively simple little message poem that traces its source to "an instantly conceived / pre-setting from wherever / Such Things Come, / and to my imagining of it . . . much a'like a teletype of / mindless source."

Indeed, Doyle's poems aren't logical discourses. They are emotional discourses, narratives of intuition with very surprising plots, in voices alternately common and "poetically" elevated.

An instance of Doyle's unpredictability is "It Is 1941 & I Am Nine Years Old All My Life," a recollection of San Fran-

---

Review of *The Collected Poems of Kirby Doyle, San Francisco Chronicle,* 1984.

cisco on the day of the attack on Pearl Harbor that hops back and forth in diction—from the vernacular to the poetical-archaic—like a bug on hot concrete: "Deathly silent th' radios / o' th' Presidio beheld / bombs fall on sunday morn . . . that day in No. Calif. . . . God, was the radio alive!"

Doyle's subjects are equally various: Here, it's Okies, Black-jack Ketchum, Thor, Buddha, Christ and the Cross, all in the same poem with Lucky Strikes, the IWW and menacing Deep Childhood Memories of Japanese invaders who "sent balloons / fill'd w' razor blades and alum powder / to blow-up / and burn over Ore. . . ."

Doyle's openness to diverse voices is a way of covering as much ground as possible. The imaginative range of his poetry repays his risks in following the interior "teletype" where it leads him. Such poems as "To say that time is running," "Satyrsong / To Dido" or "How estranged" provide meaningful tours of reality in literally inexplicable terms—moving from Point A to Point X without stopping at the in-between stations used by your average mental commuter.

Kirby Doyle's been down the street a few times. In his autobiography in Donald Allen's *New American Poetry* he recalls bluntly, "was a juvenile delinquent for the first 16 years. Am well acquainted with the insides of various police stations and minor prisons." That's also in the verse. "Myself I thought (secretly) / was John Garfield, / tough vagabond cat / punching the world right on its ass," he writes in one of his best poems, "A Speech of Me to John Kennedy." The tension between this earthy persona and the aerial raptures of imagination it nonetheless experiences—"O profound cigarette, / profounder than bells"—charges Doyle's *Collected Poems* with real electricity.

Mysteries of the Plains

Though it's sometimes very hard to locate the true article amid the disposable mass of verse litter that's constantly churned out by the nation's publishing industry, real poetry is a hardy form with great powers of endurance, capable of surviving any amount of competition from literary mediocrity.

The latest evidence of this is a first book by a twenty-nine-year-old North Dakota woman, now living in New Hampshire. She's part German, part Chippewa—her mixed roots tangling the bloodlines of the prairie's immigrant pioneers with those of its antecedent tribal residents; this intermingling seems to create the principal drama in her writing.

Her name is Louise Erdrich, and her book is called *Jacklight*. It's about the author's native-daughter experience of life in the upper Middle West, in and around the Turtle Mountain Indian Reservation, where she appears to have grown up.

This is a life her poems invest with, by turns (and sometimes at the same time), a desperate sense of the isolation enforced by geography and an ecstatic sense of the power transmitted by natural earth magic. The former sense comes across in "Walking in the Breakdown Lane," a poem about how the aching restlessness of empty space breeds a chronic longing "to be gone":

> Walking in the breakdown lane, margin of gravel,
> between the cut swaths and the road to Fargo
> I want to stop, to lie down
> in standing wheat or standing water.

Review of *Jacklight* by Louise Erdrich, *San Francisco Chronicle*, 1984.

Behind me thunder mounts as trucks of cattle
roar over, faces pressed to slats for air.
They go on, they go on without me.
They pound, pound and bawl,
and the road closes over them farther on.

As for the natural magic, it's discoverable as a trace element throughout the book, but makes its most notable appearance in the remarkable title work.

Erdrich's "jacklight" is a kind of ghostly nocturnal illumination, like marshlight or St. Elmo's fire, which in several of her poems haunts the woods and fields of the northern plains, framing the images in a backlighting of phenomenal mystery.

"Jacklight" is one of those poems that chills the heart with simultaneous dread and wonder. Its refrain, "We have come to the edge of the woods, / out of brown grass where we slept," seems to be spoken by a collective undervoice of instinct audible in many of this writer's lines—perhaps the half-mythic, half-remembered voice of her northern Ojibwa ancestors. Struck at forest edge by a wavering "fist of light" (the "night sun" or jacklight—"this battery of polarized acids that outshines the moon"), the plural speakers accept its "beams like direct blows which the heart answers" enabling them to "smell" (not see) the intrusive manifestations of a later race of settlers, with "minds like silver hammers":

It is their turn now,
their turn to follow us. Listen,
they put down their equipment.
It is useless in the tall brush.
And now they take their first steps, not knowing
how deep the woods are.

Like Wallace Stevens's "Sunday Morning," with its suggestion of the "dark encroachment" of some "old catastrophe," this poem yields a complex, diffuse burden of primordial meaning, dramatizing a clash not only of historical cultures but of states of mind, in terms at once powerful and not rationally soluble.

Poetry like this hints more than it states, proposing inescapable truths that nonetheless can't be pinned down in words other than those words it's made of. To get such work from an unheralded younger writer is a gift both gratifying and disarming. Louise Erdrich is a visitor from poetry's future, informing us, as poetry always does, that "something queer happens when the heart is delivered."

Swimming in Unknowingness

The major reputation earned by her novels *Love Medicine, The Beet Queen,* and *Tracks* has perhaps obscured the fact that it was with poetry that Louise Erdrich originally broke in—and that it's the metaphorical quality in her work, not just the storytelling, that makes her such a significant voice. It was the haunting, ecstatic earth-magic of the poems in *Jacklight,* with its powerful evocations of her youth on a northern plains Indian reservation, that landed this unheralded writer on the literary map. She has waited nearly six years to follow that promising debut with a second volume of verse. *Baptism of Desire* fulfills the promise.

Woman's submission to and participation in the rites of natural process—especially the rite of conception, pregnancy and birth, with all its mysteries, beauty, terrors and illuminations—is Erdrich's main theme in *Baptism.* It is considered multiply as spiritual commitment, biological fate and cultural role-enforcement; observed in the lives of Catholic virgin-saints of history who are given monologues, and also experienced at the first-person center of the poet's own unfolding life-drama. In a note appended to the remarkable dark-night-of-the-soul meditative sequence "Hydra," Erdrich reveals that this sequence "and most of the other poems in this book were written between the hours of three and four in the morning, a period of insomnia brought on by pregnancy."

The metaphorical "conceptions" of the saints provide backdrop for real birth trials ahead. Saint Clare, a thirteenth-

Review of *Baptism of Desire* by Louise Erdrich, *San Francisco Chronicle,* 1989.

century nun inspired to her vows by Francis of Assisi, is given a voice of mystic-ecstatic removal from self. In "The Call," Clare is transported away from the material-world prospects of family wealth and pre-arranged marriage by a vision of Christ—"seized in total night . . . I abandoned myself in his garment / like a fish in a net"—while in "My Life As a Saint," she experiences "an emptiness within me that I make lovely."

The virgin-saints' aching for spiritual fulfillment becomes in these poems a kind of self-created fate, or fatalistic submission. "Now the being rests in the bowl of my hips," speaks Erdrich's Mary in "Immaculate Conception." "There is no turning." The Virgin's participation in the mystery rite empowers her. But if the state of submission to mystery is powerful, it is also unnatural: "It was not love" that brought it about.

The Blessed Mary's "white-hot" sun of mystery vision is "a brand / that sank through me and left no mark." That translucent imprint finds ironic parallel in the spell of cultural unknowingness imposed on the contemporary woman in "Fooling God." "I must be the marrow / that he drinks into his cloud-wet body," Erdrich's submissive narrator here intones. "I must be careful and laugh when he laughs. / I must turn down the covers and guide him in. / I must fashion his children out of playdough, blue, pink, green. / I must pull them from between my legs / and set them before the television."

In "Hydra," Erdrich contemplates with analogic vision at once cosmic and cellular that "uncoiling through the length of my life" which is her unborn child—imaged as "trillium star . . . beating [its] tail across heaven," and traced back through nature's mystery to the primary "snake of the double helix," the genetic origins of being. Here it is the sheer greed of spirit to become life that breeds suffering for the sleepless mother-to-be, as she resists the fate of natural submission that has made her an only partially-willing agent in the chain of creation: "I do not want the harrow of need to pass over my body. / I do not want my children to crave me . . . ."

In the final section of *Baptism* the tensions of the drama approach resolution; the dominant chord of Erdrich's poetry, that of an instinctive acceptance of nature's unknowable mysteries, returns as a consoling harmonic, and voices of resistance and rebellion are stilled in hushed listening for new life's approach. The listening is perhaps most audible in the shimmering "Ninth Month."

This is the last month, the petrified forest
and lake which has long since turned to grass.
The sun roars over, casting its light and absence
in identical seams. One day. Another.
The child sleeps on in its capsized boat.

The hull is weathered silver and our sleep is green and dark.
Dreams of the rower, hands curled in the shape of oars
listening for the cries of alabaster birds. But all
is silent, the animals hurled into quartz.
Our bed is the wrecked blue island of time and love . . .

Black steeples, black shavings of magnetized iron,
through which the moon parades her wastes,
drawing the fruit from the female body,
pulling water like blankets up other shores.

Then slowly the sky is colored in, the snow
falls evenly into the blackness of cisterns.
The steel wings fan open that will part us from each other
and the waves break and fall according to their discipline.

Breath that moves on the waters.
Small boat, small rower.

Steel against the Dark

"We are the ones you sent to fight a war / you know nothing about." Those lines are the work of W. D. Ehrhart, a thirty-six-year-old Pennsylvanian who served as a U.S. Marine in Vietnam in 1966–67. After receiving an honorable discharge and a Purple Heart, Ehrhart became active in Vietnam Veterans Against the War, and also wrote some excellent poetry about his Vietnam experience, now collected in *To Those Who Have Gone Home Tired.*

To be more accurate, this is writing not about the war, but from it. One of the greatest gifts any writer can have is the ability to convey in a few words that complex physical reality of experience. Ehrhart possesses that gift, in rare degree. Here's his poem "One Night on Guard Duty": "The first salvo is gone before I can turn, / but there is still time to see the guns / hurl a second wave of steel against the dark. / The shells arc up, / tearing through the air like some invisible hand / crinkling giant sheets of cellophane among the stars. / The night waits, breathless, / till the far horizon erupts in brilliant / pulsing silence."

Ehrhart's poems are clear, movingly understated and beautiful because they ring so true. He is not only a combat veteran but a very fine poet—no amateur, but an accomplished practitioner, conversant with all the technical tools of his medium.

Some of Ehrhart's images remind me of the footage from the PBS documentary, "Vietnam: A Television History," on which he appeared as a central witness. It's all here—the trag-

Review of *To Those Who Have Gone Home Tired* by W. D. Ehrhart, *San Francisco Chronicle,* 1984.

edy, the waste, the blindness, the cruelty, the small and large deceits of a war fought the wrong way and for the wrong reasons. Ehrhart makes sense out of it by refusing to shy away from the senselessness at the war's heart. His honesty is not easy; it comes, often, at his own expense: "The thought occurs / that I have never hunted anything in my whole life / except other men" ("Hunting"). "In those strange Asian villages," he asks in another poem, "When they tell stories to their children / of the evil / that awaits misbehavior, / is it me they conjure?" ("Making the Children Behave").

This book should stand with Michael Herr's *Dispatches* as one of the two most vivid and involving first-hand documents of the war. Ehrhart writes about the mutuality of fear and the camaraderie of facing death but does not succumb to deceptions about heroism or patriotism. There's no sentimentalism here. "You bet we'll soon forget the one that died; / he isn't welcome any more. / He could too easily take our place / for us to think about him / any longer than it takes / to sort his personal effects . . ." ("The One That Died").

Ehrhart's Vietnam is less a place than a metaphysical state—one everybody went into alone; and those who came out, came out that way. "I cannot ever quite remember / what I went looking for, / or what it was I lost / in that alien land that became / more I / than my own can ever be again" ("To the Asian Victors"). W. D. Ehrhart's poems are a part of our national experience, a part we may not care to remember, but no less of value for that.

Lightning Bug in a Storm

The life of Ramon Guthrie (1896–1973) was unusual even for a poet. Born in poverty in New York, fatherless from early youth, raised by a Christian Scientist dressmaker who occasionally farmed him out to an orphanage, he volunteered for service in the First World War, where he drove an ambulance on the Western Front, survived a spectacular air crash and later won a Silver Star for heroic exploits with a bomber squadron.

After hospitalization in America for service injuries, Guthrie returned to France where, with his French wife, he spent much of the next decade as an expatriate writer, living in Montparnasse and associating with Pound, Hemingway, Giacometti and Sinclair Lewis (who became a close friend). By 1930, he was an expert in French literature, a subject he taught at Dartmouth College for the next thirty-three years. These years were also occupied with writing, painting, translating, visiting France on sabbaticals and serving, during World War II, with the OSS and the French Resistance.

In 1963, Guthrie retired from Dartmouth and began concentrating on his poetry. Three years later he underwent surgery for bladder cancer, the beginning of a seven-year medical ordeal that later included many more surgeries and hospitalizations, the removal of his colon, Parkinson's disease, asthma, double vision, severe hallucinations. During this period of torment that would have killed the creative

Review of *Maximum Security Ward and Other Poems* by Ramon Guthrie, edited by Sally M. Gall, *San Francisco Chronicle*, 1984.

spirit of a lesser man, Guthrie produced his masterpiece, a long poetic sequence, *Maximum Security Ward.*

This forty-nine-poem work, really a single poem in many interrelating movements, remains one of the most—if not *the* most—affecting tributes in American literature to the survival of human dignity in the face of extreme adversity. The "ward" of the title was actually an intensive care unit where, with courage, wit and irony summoned up from God-knows-what amazing reservoirs, Guthrie spent hour after hour writing, filling the long, slow times before the arrival of each bleak new hospital day. "Not dawn yet," was Guthrie's way of telling time in these poems. (One of his few complaints is that his watch had been taken away from him.)

The predictable, appalling details of physical humiliation and suffering take up very little of *Maximum Security Ward.* They are there, but only as a kind of negative backdrop, a challenge that Guthrie used to drive himself along on his real purpose, which was celebration, through memory, of those graces of body and soul that he proposed as barriers against death's permanent dominion. Through the personae of troubadour poets and pastoral shepherds, cave painters, musicians, artists, aviators, lovers—the "christoi," or anointed ones, who have chosen to be or been chosen as creative spirits—he constructed a timeless world in defiance of his very mortal, immediate present-tense surroundings. "The dead are very near," he wrote, "They move freely / We talk together with no / need of words."

The writing is as full of hallucination as it is of recollection, as much laced with vision as with the literal imagery of bygone experience. Guthrie's mind floated out of his body and away from his hospital bed: "I have come back having grasped perhaps as much / as a lightning bug, clinging through a storm / to a leaf's underside, / might understand by fellow-feeling / of the lightning stroke that in a single blast / has ripped the elm trunk all its length."

Composed out of delirium and ecstatic black humor, hopeless gaiety and the exultation of resignation beyond grief, *Maximum Security Ward* is a poem to be ranked not only with the work of Guthrie's contemporaries—Williams, Stevens, Pound—but with the literature of spiritual illumination, works such as St. John of the Cross's *Dark Night of the Soul,* and Tolstoy's *The Death of Ivan Ilyich.*

Peanuts and Allusion

This poem functions like a Lysol aerosol spray aimed at "a fungus of some / criminal type." It satirizes that extended cocktail party, the Modern Language Association Convention, an annual gathering of the national linguistic professoriat ("several thousand babblers").

This particular meeting took place in 1981 at the Houston Hyatt House, whose "blank amplitude of nonentity" and "rows of trees, covered with stars the size of peas" and painted "counterfeit green," provide an appropriately contemporary backdrop for cultural satire.

Houston—or "Hughestown," as Edward Dorn terms it in honor of the man whose empire was founded there—is the fastest-growing city in the West. Once a rank swamp flat, it is now the business capital of that whole stretch of America between the Mississippi and the Pacific, the region that this poet has long made his specific subject.

It's the same terrain where once prevailed the archetypal gambler-gunfighter figure, that radical, mythological, independent, itinerant freethinker celebrated by Dorn in his sixties mock-epic *Gunslinger.*

In this new poem, the West has become capital-intensive, the gunslinger and even the wildcatter (etched into the Dorn legend in the tale "C. B. & Q.") have been replaced by new denizens in "Dark suits, almost abstract pinstripes" instead of rawhide chaps, toting cocktails and briefcases instead of six-guns or drill rigs.

Review of *Captain Jack's Chaps or Houston/MLA* by Edward Dorn, *San Francisco Chronicle,* 1984.

"It's no longer possible even to exist at survival level in the West without making the kind of money that used to qualify one as wealthy," this poet has said. *Captain Jack's Chaps* proposes sugar as the dominant cultural metaphor. Beef was once the solid foundation of the West. Now it's something much more basic—the credit card.

"Sugar is the red meat of the vegetarian diet," Dorn writes. Between the lines, in the "elongated bunkers" of the Houston Hyatt, sugar and lucre are interchangeable, the brilliant sweetening which is a substitute for protein, just as academic jargon and computer-programming are substitutes for thought.

"Where's the beef?" is the question Dorn seems to be asking of the higher education system whose communication specialists are gathered here at the convention. Their reply is "Peanuts and Allusion, / brie and Reference," bobbing atop the muzak-y, "sugary beat of calypso" and "oceans of smugness" that swell "round and round the cocktail well" of the Hyatt.

Dorn's overview of Western history is that of a series of migratory waves, the last of which has merged in "a grand migratory effect . . . This whole thing is being ruled by Texas. This is the Texas nation . . . everybody should stop kidding themselves, and forget California . . . now it's Texas. And it goes all the way to Alaska."

To this poet-historian, the washing-up of the modern language professors, "spewing gratuities" at the Houston Hyatt, is one quintessential droplet of the Last Wave. Beyond lies mere quantity and exhaustion. The sugary technical taste of this brilliant, vacant present, with its radical proposition of the absolute emptying-out of language by those responsible for it in our nation's institutions, makes up the comic content of one of the few major American satirical poems of recent times.

Outlaw Metaphysics

Gunslinger, Edward Dorn's anti-post-industrial-capitalist mock-epic of the contemporary West, was conceived and initiated in 1967 and issued serially in five separate small press volumes over the next several years. The present edition makes the whole poem available for the first time since a 1975 compilation went out of print.

It's a fine time for the revival of this brilliant, challenging and prophetic work. Also an ironically appropriate one. In the so-called "Geezer Summer" just past, we've had paraded before us, in various states of preservation, many of the surviving hulks of a once vibrant sixties pop culture. Not that the return of Mick and Keith, Pete and Roger, Elton and Stevie and Ringo, hasn't been fun, but unfortunately even the nostalgia wave hasn't been enough to overcome the crow's feet and advancing paunches, the obvious ebbing of energies.

Gunslinger, happily, has aged far better.

Dorn's ambitious, inventive, multi-voiced allegorical narrative plays off pop song and cowboy ballad to assemble an outrageous outlaw metaphysics, extravagantly updating pre-Socratic philosophies and the myths of comic book gunman and Hollywood / TV frontier hero to fit the subjectivist ethics of the Vietnam War era drug culture. ("To a poet all authority / except his own / is an expression of Evil.")

Good guys in this moral fable are a weird little traveling band of stoned pilgrims, including the Slinger himself, a 2000-year-old "son of the sun"; his delightful dance-hall-madam companion Cocaine Lil, "a Girl from the montaine /

Review of *Gunslinger* by Edward Dorn, *San Francisco Chronicle*, 1989.

raised on air and light"; and his "Stoned Horse," a shamelessly anthropomorphized, ultramodern steed who grazes on the kind of grass that's rolled into giant "Tampico Bombers."

Their collective mission is a trek to Las Vegas to confront the techno-entrepreneurial "Shortage Industry" captained by the poem's arch-villain, Howard Hughes, a latter-day robber baron intent on "hustling the future" with his "enchanted Wallet." But the picaresque voyage up the Rio Grande Valley from the Mexican border is never completed. The goal of Las Vegas, like the dominant rational discourse system with which the poem continually tilts, proves a "vast decoy"; the travelers get only as far as the Colorado Plateau, here a paradisal landscape of high, dry spaces, time-carved rock and ecstatic light.

The point of their trip after all, it's gradually revealed, was the journey itself: "To See / is their desire / as they wander," writes Dorn. A drifter-poet who joins the group en route, producing pure songs to the instrumental accompaniment of an "abso-lute," becomes the author's most effective lyric mouthpiece, expansively evoking the awesome landforms of the American Cordillera in a wild, neo-cosmological, shot-from-the-hip verse metric.

"The journalist has got tomorrow as his main habit," poet Dorn once remarked in comparing his own art to the more topically immediate mode of reportage, with its necessary addiction to the historical moment. "As a poet, you're always writing against all the time you need. Poetry seeks to incandesce for a longer period, but it's news anyway."

Gunslinger has indeed stayed news. This engaging extended narrative comes across today as just as speedy, angular, subversive, eloquent, uplifting and funny as it was twenty years ago. And its principal satiric premise—"Entrapment is this society's / sole activity . . . Only laughter / can blow it to rags"—may now be more relevant than ever.

Stalin as Linguist—I

This epidemical conspiracy for the destruction of paper.
—Dr. Johnson

It is easier to think what Poetry should be than to write it—and this
leads me on to another axiom. That if Poetry comes not as naturally
as the Leaves to a tree it had better not come at all . . . We hate
poetry that has a palpable design upon us . . . The Genius of Poetry
must work out its own salvation in a man: It cannot be matured by
law & precept, but by sensation & watchfulness in itself—That
which is creative must create itself . . .
—John Keats

"How do you spell language?"
"Without the 'I.'"
(First of the Language School "Knock Knock" jokes.)
—Tom Raworth

I got a call from Richard Silberg, one of the editors of *Poetry Flash*. "We're running a big article about the language poets," Richard said. "We'd like you to write a response for next month's *Flash*." He summarized the article for me. I thought, "Oh no . . ." I said, "Okay, tell me what you need."

Richard laid down three ground rules. "No personal abuse . . . No *argumentum ad hominem* . . . And no bringing down demonic energies."

If I was good enough to bring down demonic energies, I thought to myself, I wouldn't have to do journalism to make a living. "Don't worry about a thing," I told Richard.

His other two ground rules bothered me slightly more, however. How do you talk about a question which after all primarily concerns the society of poets (who else cares about it?) without acknowledging you're a member of that society

---

Poetry Flash, 1985.

yourself, i.e., a person in a community of allegedly like-inclined persons?

"Personal history yes," I decided. "Personal abuse no."

As for *argumentum ad hominem*—I suspected that might prove a particularly difficult pitfall to avoid. Once I'd actually read the article I'd been assigned to reply to, this suspicion deepened into a profound certainty. An *ad hominem* argument, as we all know, is one that takes advantage of the character or situation of a particular opponent. Using the opponent's own words or acts as evidence in support of your case. After I'd worked my way through the piece in question—a real labor in itself—Richard's *ad hominem* prohibition came to look like an impassable barrier.

But I'm going to try to be logical about all this nonetheless.

Let's start with a logical question. The article, "On Whose Authority?," is written by a UC linguistics professor, George Lakoff; it addresses at length various subjects related to poetry. I'm told (by editor Silberg) that Prof. Lakoff was invited by the *Flash* to write this article, the first in what's to be a series of in-depth pieces on current poetics. Prof. Lakoff's credentials, as stated by the *Flash:* "His expertise is in the theory of grammar and the theory of meaning." Now the logical question is, why would a *linguist* be writing an article about *poetry*?

One of the big claims of the language poets is that they're "deconditioning language," i.e., exterminating double-talk, jargon, and the like. One wonders, then, how they feel about having as advocate a career academic whose "expertise" tempts him constantly into the slough of pretentious professional jargon and double-bubble-lingo-babble? Here's Prof. Lakoff in action: "A frame is a conceptual organization that makes sense of some area of experience . . . The linguist who has studied this the most is my colleague, Charles Fillmore, who has argued that word meaning and grammatical meaning in general is tied to framing . . ." etc. Lakoff's style is typical academic linguistic-speak, bristling with "signifieds" and "signifiers," "interactions" and "taxonomies," "receivers" and "decoders"—a confident professionalist drone lethal as the Andromeda Strain when unleashed on poetry.

Prof. Lakoff may be an "expert" in his specialty—theoretical linguistics—but whether he knows it or not, there's more to poetry than formalist theory. His article evinces little knowledge of poetry, in fact. His summary dismissal of pre-"language" poetry as "packaged literary tours" is both vague and condescending. He speaks with patronizing contempt of the "romantic ideal" of the poetry of the past, according to which, he notes, "poetry was to serve an uplifting and healing function by communicating deep truths in especially charged, compact form." This is a fallacy, he claims—and, he tells us sadly, one that's "still with us." His goal is to dispel it, by explaining that "what is great in great poetry is not its referential content." (He neglects to inform us what *is*, in fact, "great in great poetry.") His high-handed devaluation of everything that came before Carla Harryman (evidently his favorite contemporary writer; he compares her with Wittgenstein!) reaches its peak in his comments on the work of Charles Olson, whose "historical frame," he blithely suggests, "eventually took over the entire work and became boring."

It's worth pausing at this point to consider the whole question of the relation between poetry and the specialized rhetoric of theoretical linguistics. The kind of approach used by George Lakoff is, of course, very similar to the one the language poets use in addressing themselves. The "work" of language poets consists largely of self-reflexive formalist theorizing. It's like the girl on the Dutch cleanser box who looks in the Dutch cleanser box at the girl on the Dutch cleanser box who looks . . . Asked (in a recent issue of *Poetry Flash*) his opinion of the actual poetic production of the language poets, Allen Ginsberg commented gently that they're "long on theory," which is an understatement akin to saying a calculator is long on numbers.

George Lakoff thinks this is just wonderful. To him, the language poets' poems are almost afterthoughts to the theories anyway. His article has the ostensible purpose of reviewing the volume *Writing/Talks*, a handbook of language school "talks." With such books as this, *The L-A-N-G-U-A-G-E Book*, *Code of Signals* and *Total Syntax*, he says, language "talks" have been "institutionalized as a genre." (Institutionalization is here implicitly viewed as a positive—i.e., it goes without saying that the current state of the "genre" is better than its pre-institutionalized condition.) This "institutionalizing" of "talks" is a revolutionary gesture, Lakoff contends, like "workers taking over a factory." By "institutionalizing" their "talks," the worker-poets "serve the needs of their community." The key word here is *their*, not *yours* or *mine* or *his*. (Lakoff makes it clear that he's not one of "them"; he admires their "worthwhile enterprise" from a safe distance, and "enjoys reading about it.")

And *how*, specifically, do the "talks" serve the needs of "their" community? By allowing the poets to seize "authority," heretofore appropriated by "critics" (the implication here is that all critics outside "their community" are uninformed, therefore hostile). No longer can critics criticize the language poets, George Lakoff tells us; the poets criticize themselves. They have wrested away "the power of characterization." The "self-characterization" of their "talks," he proclaims, "is what the movement is about." "It is about the rejection of authority and control . . . the authority and control of the literary establishment." These language poets of Prof. Lakoff's now possess "real sex organs" as well as "brains"; they are "free citizens" who "need to be able to create for themselves the meanings of events." (A short aside from personal history: when the language school rejects the authority of "outside" critics it doesn't kid around! This writer recently had the temerity to review Barrett Watten's *Total Syntax*. The published review was taped to the display window at Small Press Distribution in Berkeley. Hearing it was there, Watten raced in, tore it down and ripped it up. *Sic transit* freedom of opinion.)

"Self-characterizing," George Lakoff believes, is the great triumph of language writers. Of *Writing/Talks*, he says, "In a sense, this entire volume is an exercise in self-characterization by the language poets collectively. Interestingly enough, much of it is out in the open, as in the cases where poets interpret their own poems."

It's especially "out in the open" in Bob Perelman's "Sense," one of the "talks" in *Writing/Talks*. Perelman here unashamedly exposes a considerable skill for self-characterizing. He reads passages of his poetry, then talks about them. We hear how he's used Jakobson, Saussure, Shelley, Jung, Piaget, the *Scientific American,* Quintillian, Gildersleeve's *Latin Grammar,* Robert Smithson, Jean Cohen, and other writers and thinkers, in constructing his works. "The lines are actually from a . . . horror movie, 'The Brain' . . . This poem is really about high school sex. . . ." and so on. "I guess I'm going to stop," Perelman tells us at one point, "and, every time I think of something, I'm going to say it."

Once upon a time it may have been considered arrogant, immodest, or plain silly for a writer to obtrude his explications of his work upon his audience—to whom, putatively, he owes a certain debt of gratitude for their willingness to sit still and read/hear his work in the first place. But with language school writers, self-explication is not only permissible, it's *de rigueur.* This is, Lakoff insists, a sign of their "democratic, anti-elitist" stance. And indeed there *is* a yawning egalitarianism to it. I'll tell you how I made *my* works, you tell me how you made *yours . . .*

"Self-characterization" goes on not only in the "talks" but in the poems which are extensions of them. Take Barrett Watten's *Progress,* a recently published long poem which is evidently an extended commentary upon itself and the compositional act that produced it. Some sample stanzas: "The business of art is surface / And its extent. / *Place I* / Pronouns in the middle of / Enhanced perception of depth . . ." "All information ends in a book. / Blindness, / write anything / And arrange to follow sound / As an imitation of zeitgeist . . ." "One way contradictory use is to / Specify empty. / Basis, its / Cover operates under insist on, / Delineate. Stalin as a linguist . . ." Priggish to a fault, self-reflexive, variably articulate, mock-professorial, *Progress* is a solipsist tour de force. (Mr. Watten's worship of Victor Shklovsky can be glimpsed in the backdrop, like a small flame guttering on a tiny altar. Shklovsky's dictum of "estrangement," or distancing, provides rationale for Watten's disjunctive mode, which resembles Shklovsky's own work about as much as a bluefly resembles a blue whale. Shklovsky wrote about the major events of the twentieth century—the Russian Revolution and its aftermath; he went from writing to assembling armored cars. Watten writes about the inside of his head;

he goes from writing to copyediting texts for the University of California.)

But "self-characterizing" isn't something the language poets invented. If Prof. Lakoff knew anything about literary history, he'd know the self-congratulatory poetic address is a phenomenon as old as the first outcroppings of academic verse dilettantism. Swift wrote about it best, in his satire *A Tale of a Tub:*

> I hold myself obliged to give as much light as is possible, into the beauties and excellencies of what I am writing, because it is become the fashion and humor most applauded among the first authors of this polite and learned age, when they would correct the ill nature of the critical, or inform the ignorance of courteous readers. Besides, there have been several famous pieces lately published both in verse and prose, wherein, if the writers had not been pleased, out of their great humanity and affection to the public, to give us a nice detail of the sublime and the admirable they contain, it is a thousand to one whether we should ever have discovered one grain of either . . . I here think fit to lay hold on that great and honorable privilege of being the last writer. I claim an absolute authority in right, as the freshest Modern, which gives me a despotic power over all authors before me . . . Our great Dryden . . . has often said to me in confidence, that the world would have never suspected him to be so great a poet, if he had not assured them so frequently in his prefaces, that it was impossible they could either doubt or forget it.

Every age has its "freshest Moderns." The brilliant satire of *A Tale of a Tub* and *The Battle of the Books* punctured the over-inflated, self-important "modernity" of mediocre writers whose real claim to significance was nothing more than the accidental fact that they came *after* everything that had *gone before.* The strategic advantage of the language school, and its imperious attitude, are based on a similar claim; but today there are no Swifts around to take its measure.

Once recognized, any avant garde is always overrated by academies. The academic view of literary history is channeled through a stereopticon of temporal distortion. Pound, Joyce and Eliot were "moderns." Then along came the "post-moderns." Suddenly the "moderns" themselves were pushed back into the bulky continuum of history. Such relative labelling is an academic convenience useful to dull categorists like the MLA (where, by the way, there's currently a flurry of interest in the language school). In fifty years (or twenty, or ten, or five) today's avant garde will be pushed back into the past, where it will join the grand democracy of extant literature. A writer like Barrett Watten will take his place in literary history alongside other great flukes. Thomas Chatterton was once the avant garde.

The language school didn't just grow, like Topsy. Their formalist aesthetic came out of French structuralism. Their procedural modes as practicing poets come out of the New York school. They have a well-documented love-hate relationship with the New York school; it's proverbial that children often claim to hate their fathers.

Personal aside: Alastair Johnston and I were talking about "language writing." I proposed that these writers have got a lot of mileage out of New York school retreads. "Yes," said Alastair. "But these guys get all uptight, spend fifty hours sweating and laboring to construct the same kind of meaningless gibberish that people used to smoke a joint and produce in ten minutes—and then they say, 'Wow, look at this,' as though nobody's ever done it before."

Of course, for language school uses, New York models have to be re-processed, de-personalized, so as to fit better into a technological future. A future in which discourse is terminated, and all that's left of language are the fragmented inarticulate remains, a non-referential solipsist muzak.

Language school writing is very industrial strength, "long on theory," short on feeling. Prof. Lakoff brings up the "passions" of the language writers—three times, in fact. Perhaps he's talking about those famous "real sex organs" of theirs; certainly there's no passion in the *writing*. I have read more of their work than I've cared to, and I've found it consistently over-cerebralized and absolutely lacking in the kind of formal transposition of emotion which good poetry—or good writing—always possesses.

Emotion comes from *emovere,* to *move out.* The first sign of life is movement. Writing possessed by the fire of imagination is writing that *moves.* The heat of this divine possession is something *felt.* Life is combustion. The heart has no back burners. Its movements are *out front* (directional). To remove heat and emotion from writing is to simulate the *language of machines.* Machine talk is cool and static, the technological communication of asteroid dwellers.

(What's dull, depressing and predictable about today's techno-consumer society is its arrogant claim that machines can not only replace the working of the human heart, soul and spirit, but they can *do a better job.* I don't believe it.)

Technology is the death of humor. Machines don't get the joke. Neither does language school criticism. Here is Barrett Watten in *Total Syntax* (writing about his wife):

> . . . there is often, in certain writers, a borrowing of alternate total forms with values entirely different from those of the totalizing present, to be used in the construction of a work. Narrative or expository tags from other genres shift the present from the totality being asserted to a synthetic and more possible whole. Carla Harryman indicates such a use of another total form in the values she gives in her work to the genre of detective fiction, in terms of a condensation not unlike that in Shklovsky . . .

Questions: What is "a more possible whole"? (Try to imagine a "less possible whole.") What is "the totalizing present"? And was Watten's last sentence written as an entry in a contest (bonuses for each additional prepositional phrase beginning with "in")?

Language school criticism is an insect-like analytical method that's ultimately blunted by the inability of those who employ it to think or write clearly. A writer who's all thumbs can never point a finger at anything. By definition whatever such a writer writes will be non-referential because accuracy of reference is continually escaping. For such a writer to celebrate non-referentiality (as all "language" writers do, much to the joy of Prof. Lakoff) is a case of the very common condition of reverse envy. A person who does something badly feels compelled to devalue the skill he or she lacks.

With language writers, skill is replaced by mutual reinforcement. Group support can turn a deficiency into an advantage by developing shared convictions and consensus statements of value. In a totally consenting group any proposition will be universally endorsed, even an absurd one—e.g., the proposition that baffling, opaque clots of language have a redeeming value in and for "the community." It may strike the casual observer as surprising that language writers commonly assert the "communal" or "social" value of their work. It may be suggested that linguistic solipsism is in fact not of much use to the majority of people. The majority of people aren't invited to the language school party. A large—but of course invisible—sign over the door reads: "Specialists only." (In the age of technological specialization, this is only appropriate.)

But a cohesive mutual support group can convince itself of any outlandish proposition by means of simple group consent. Consensus is truth. If language school writers, who aspire to academia, don Yuppie trappings and share materialistic Yuppie goals—thus aligning themselves socially with an "elitist" group—care to think of themselves as leftists, no one ought to be surprised. The shared mutual convictions of any closed society reflect the needs of the group very accurately, thus serving as symptomatic indicators rather than objective statements. (Self-characterization *uber alles!*)

But make no mistake. The language school's campaign *is* political. They simply intend to conquer the scene *en bloc*.

Poets have traditionally been individualists. Language school writers prefer safety in numbers. Their "talks" are sermons preached to the converted. An "outsider" has a hard time making sense of them. The reactions of outsiders are of no interest to language school writers except insofar as said outsiders are seen as potential sources of power. Literary power, and the seizure of same, is obviously a principal desideratum of the language school. Once again, the sheer power of numbers comes into play. The block "takeover" of a magazine, a reading venue, or a publishing concern, is seen as a "victory" comparable to a battlefield success. Differences of opinion are not encouraged, any more than quarreling is encouraged between soldiers engaged in a common military struggle. The military analogy is very useful in understanding language school tactics. The Bay Area is their greatest beachhead to date, a kind of Normandy of Dullness.

> *See! still thy own, the heavy cannon roll,*
> *And metaphysic smokes involve the pole.*
> *For thee we dim the eyes and stuff the head*
> *With all such reading as was never read:*
> *For thee explain a thing till all men doubt it,*
> *And write about it, goddess, and about it:*
> *So spins the silk-worm small its slender store,*
> *And labours till it clouds itself all o'er.*
> *—Alexander Pope, Aristarchus's address*
> *to the Goddess Dullness, from* The Dunciad

Seen as part of history—I mean social history, not just literary history—the emergence of a gang mentality among writers in an age of general social fragmentation is only to be expected. In our time it's common for persons of submissive character to gather around powerful, dominant personalities. Social groupings disguised as art movements can be included in this. Locally in the Bay Area, the language school is a social grouping first of all, one which has formed, or coalesced, or *agglutinated*—I want a *colloidal* metaphor here, conveying a certain post-vertebrate flocculence, as of egg whites floating in water—around particular autocratic figures.

"It's characteristic of the state of the nation," local writer Bob Grenier has recently said of the language school, "that people form these defensive, aggressive groups." Behind such a comment lies an obvious artistic distrust for such unanimity as a "school" implies; it's no accident that a writer as stubbornly unreconstructed as Grenier finds himself occasionally in the language doghouse.

The language school has had considerably less trouble keeping in line such other writers of Grenier's generation as have proven convenient to their program.

Co-opting the generation of poets prior to Grenier's poses even fewer problems. The name "Robert Creeley" has begun to appear under laudatory statements on the backs of Barrett Watten's books. Creeley is a great poet whose critical discriminations have proven chronically subject to velleities of personal affection—to the point where we get the image of him as the blind bishop, proffering his ring to be kissed by whatever young poet's next in line. And then there are a lot of dead poets, who are easy to co-opt because they can't fight back. Zukofsky, Olson, Spicer and Berrigan are examples of writers who, through no fault of their own, became instant language school antecedents simply by dying.

Consider for example, Watten's uses of Charles Olson: first nervously defensive, then increasingly proprietary, in progressive stages of critical resuscitation—through which Olson is gradually shorn of what Watten terms his "bigness," i.e., his expressionist tendencies, "paternalist psychology," and "wall of sound" (not to mention the "historical frame" which Prof. Lakoff finds so "boring"). Watten's generous rescue of Olson hinges on a deft juggling of pseudo-categories: Big O's "*linguistic* present created," Watten finally allows, "far outweighs" his objectionable "in-time romance of self"; *ergo* Olson is permitted to stand as a linear antecedent of Watten & Co. (and that large quake you hear is Olson turning over in his grave to see a quote from *Maximus* as the epigraph page of Watten's *Progress*).

A similar reductivist laundering of Ted Berrigan was conducted by Watten's colleague Charles Bernstein, who waited less than a year after Berrigan stopped breathing to lasso him into a tidy formalist corral. This was done in an article wherein Bernstein "showed" that the terms of person, body, self and autobiography did *not* play a primary role in the creation of Berrigan's poems.

An Olson without soul and a Berrigan without heart fit nicely into language school canons.

Swift wrote about all this in *The Battle of the Books*. In Swift's account, Virgil—for whom we might read, say, "Olson"—appears in shining armor, casting his eye over the battlefield in search of an adversary worthy of his valor. A mounted foe appears, but as this cavalier draws closer, instead of engaging in combat, he lifts up the visor of his helmet and requests a parlay. The Modern cavalier is Dryden (or Watten?). Virgil is startled, "as one possessed with surprise and disappointment altogether": Dryden's helmet is "nine times too large for the head." Thereupon the pinheaded Modern proceeds to utter "a long harangue." "He soothed up the good Ancient, called him father, and by a large deduction of genealogies, made it plainly appear that they were nearly related. Then he humbly proposed an exchange of armor." Virgil consents—"for the goddess Diffidence came unseen, and cast a mist before his eyes"—and trades his gold armor for the Modern's rusty iron. "However, this glittering armor became the Modern yet worse than his own." Then they agree to exchange horses. "But when it came to the trial, Dryden was afraid, and utterly unable to mount . . ."

Swift is one writer whose work would seem invulnerable to lingo-scholastic co-optation, but then again you never know.

Stalin as Linguist—II

"To write poetry now, even on current events, means to withdraw into the ivory tower. It's as though one were practicing the art of filigree. There is something eccentric, cranky, obtuse about it. Such poetry is like the castaway's note in the bottle."

Though it's been almost forty-five years since Bertolt Brecht made that statement, it has never been more applicable than at present; poets have never seemed more "eccentric, cranky, obtuse," their poems never fuller of the consummate irrelevance implied by Brecht's phrase, "the art of filigree." In what is obviously an extremely fragmented time for society at large as well as for the special interests of literature, the arts have entered a phase of extreme "pluralization"—as Ron Silliman, editor of the new "language poetry" anthology, *In the American Tree,** calls it. All thoughts of truth or beauty or *quality* in writing are to be considered either nostalgic or plain reactionary, or so Silliman implies. "Any debate over who is, or is not a better writer," he decrees in his introduction, "is, for the most part, a surrogate social struggle."

The guidebooks to this brave new world beyond the who's-a-better-writer debate are starting to roll off not only the small presses—among which the "language" movement has already implanted itself—but those of some of America's universities as well. In recent years Southern Illinois University Press has issued some of the principal documents of this movement,

Partisan Review, 1987.
* *In the American Tree,* edited by Ron Silliman (Orono, Me.: National Poetry Foundation, University of Maine, 1986).

including Barrett Watten's volume of critical essays (*Total Syntax*) and Bob Perelman's collection of those shadowboxing, self-qualifying "talks" which are this group's dominant mode of production (*Writing/Talks*). Now, from the University of Maine's National Poetry Foundation, comes this six-hundred-odd-page blockbuster anthology, a volume that registers the movement's literary performance to date.

The "language school," as this group is often called (in honor of *L-A-N-G-U-A-G-E*, a magazine Silliman terms "the first American journal of poetics by and for poets"), has its stronghold in the San Francisco Bay Area, where its major movers (including Watten, Silliman, Perelman, and Lyn Hejinian) are based. There is also a New York branch, whose most prominent poet is Charles Bernstein. While there is a certain diversity of style among all these writers *as* writers, they display a surprising unanimity of purpose as evidenced in the critical writings and statements which take up a good one-third of *In the American Tree*. As avant-garde movements go, this one has exhibited a rare degree of cohesiveness (if not coherence). Silliman, in his introduction, traces the beginnings of the movement back to 1971, when Watten, as cofounder with Robert Grenier of *This* magazine, proclaimed a departure from the "speech-based poetics" of William Carlos Williams, Charles Olson and Robert Creeley, and suggested a move toward a new, "non-referential" procedure, which would build poems not from "images, not voice, not characters or plot," but "only through the invocation of a specific medium, language itself." This anthology, Silliman says, "documents what became of that suggestion."

This new non-referential "axis" (as Silliman calls it) proposed a "public discourse on poetics" to replace the disorder and confusion of avant-garde poetic generations immediately prior to it—the Beats, the Black Mountain "projectivists," the New York School. All of those were represented in Donald Allen's *New American Poetry* (1960), and Silliman draws a bead on that anthology here, as though it were a principal obstacle in the path of his movement. According to him, there was one major problem with all of them: their failure to produce enough "criticism."

The language school writers will never be guilty of *that*. They are as long on critical theory as they are (relatively, and I think also absolutely) short on poems. Their criticism is mostly written in a pretentious intellectual *argot* that sounds a little like an assistant professor who took a wrong turn on the way to the Derrida Cookout and ended up at the poetry reading. What poetry they do write is mostly an odd alloy of the methodology of all that critical prose and the models of their "disorderly" literary predecessors. The voices of Creeley and John Ashbery, to name two powerful influences, are clearly audible in the background of some of the better poems here—Creeley behind Robert Grenier's, say, and Ashbery behind Charles Bernstein's. Another kind of voice, more constructivist than expressionist in its origins, can be heard in the work of Watten and Silliman, who base their writings on programmatic principles of composition. But the poets in all these strains share a reflexive quality, and their work has a tendency to talk about itself, sometimes in a language reminiscent of technical manuals, as in Watten's poem "Position":

> The apex settles on
>
> Tones in surrounding heads.
>   A test case, or
> exile. No wires account for
> failure of specific response.
>   A triangle gives,
> circles branch out. Forced
>
> Exposure to limit distorts. . . .

Watten's critical prose, also amply represented here, deploys the same kind of institutional-gray vocabulary to only slightly different ends. In his prose Watten seems to owe a debt to the distancing and disjunction methods of the Russian Formalists, especially Viktor Shklovsky. His interest in Shklovsky reflects the leftist stance that's common among language school writers. One critic, Fred Pollack, has suggested that "language-school leftism is either stupid or disingenuous, the icing on a cake only bourgeois intellectuals can afford." Indeed, solidarity among the language school cadres is expressed not in bomb-throwing or plotting the overthrow of the state but in tactics like letter-writing campaigns, such as the one Watten orchestrated when I criticized his work in *Poetry Flash* recently.

To give some background: My first foray into criticism of the language school was in a January 1985 *San Francisco Chronicle* review of Watten's *Total Syntax,* wherein I took issue with, among other things, his terminology (Watten seems unable to get to the end of a sentence without tripping over an "obscured referent" or "grammatical completion" along the way), and suggested such writing was "the kind of mumbo jumbo you'd hear from a guy who stumbled into a linguistics lecture one day, and walked out an instant expert the next." The *Chronicle* received a storm of angry letters from Watten's allies, including one from his erstwhile Ph.D. adviser, who called me a "reactionary frump." That same letter-writer, a well-known University of California linguistics professor named George Lakoff, also produced an article later the same year for the local poetry periodical *Poetry Flash.* Titled "On Whose Authority?," the article's central point was that "language" writers had seized back (from "outside" critics) the "authority" to "characterize" their own work (in their "talks," statements, manifestoes, etc.). To Lakoff these writers were acting not like your average yuppified literary careerists (whom they resembled to some "outsiders") but like revolutionary "workers" who'd "taken over the factory."

Anyway, the editors of *Poetry Flash* must have felt a little anxious about Lakoff's article, because they asked me to write a response. (This assignment, Watten later suggested, amounted to my being "used" as a "bad-guy figure" by the devious and cunning *Flash* editors.) My response was called "Stalin as Linguist." The title was taken from a passage in Watten's poem, *Progress.* The passage read: "One way contradictory use is to / Specify empty. / Basis, its / Cover operates under insist on, / Delineate. Stalin as a linguist . . . ." The title probably caused as much furor as the article itself.

Watten reacted by composing a two-page, single-spaced, indignant, "not-for-publication" communiqué to *Poetry Flash.* The letter demanded redress of grievances and threatened a boycott by advertisers. Attached was a list of people to receive copies. The list was almost as long as the letter itself. It contained the names of language school sympathizers with influential positions—institutional poetry administrators, reading coordinators, publishers, book distributors, bookstore owners and employees, university teachers, gallery representatives, etc. From these people and from others in the language school's local rank and file, *Poetry Flash* received a flood of letters. A selection appeared in subsequent issues of the paper. Several correspondents, such as Robert Gluck of the San Francisco State Poetry Center, charged me with "red-baiting." Joe McCarthy was evoked more than once, as were the "mau-maus" (by Silliman, though that letter never made it into print).

All of this suggests that despite its dedication to the *ideal* of criticism as equal in importance to creative work, the language school has a very thin skin when it comes to *taking* criticism. In the minds of Watten and other theorists of this movement—or at least in their pronunciamentos—the movement itself is nothing less than a forward surge of the great Hegelian dialectic of history. Any "outside" critic is forced into the role of reactionary. Hence the outraged tone of their plaints about "language-bashing." "Attacks have been made on this writing," Silliman says in his introduction. "No other current poetic tendency in America has been subjected to anything like the constant flow of dismissals and exposes [*sic*], many of them composed in the threatened rhetoric of fury, as have the poets here."

Silliman attributes such "dismissals" and "exposes" to the anachronistic persistence of "a simple ego psychology" dependent on such outmoded bourgeois values as "communication" and "emotion"—thus setting the stage for a familiar language school morality play: persecution and martyrdom at the hands of the right wing. Shortly after my *Poetry Flash* article appeared, a former director of the San Francisco State Poetry Center (this fellow made a name for himself locally by staging language school events) sent me a postcard with an X-rated cartoon on the front and a message that charged me, in no uncertain terms, with being "right in there weenie-to-weenie with Reagan and the Pope safeguarding those Western Judeo-

Christian verities," and even of being in the "pay" of "the Vatican"!

It's been pointed out more than once that the tyranny of method over material in the language writers' work and of group unanimity over individual variation in their political strategizing add up to the very thing they pretend to abhor most, a sad authoritarianism. But who or what is on the left and who or what on the right? In the administered world of the present, as Theodor Adorno has said, "all works of art including radical ones have a conservative image, for they help reinforce the existence of a separate domain of spirit and culture whose practical impotence and complicity with the principle of unmitigated disaster are painfully evident." The phrase "including radical ones" points up the meaninglessness of current "left" vs. "right" arguments on aesthetic issues.

These writers' claim to social value is not that they are building a discourse but breaking one down. They have informed us repeatedly that they are "de-constructing" language, "defamiliarizing" it, even (as one "language" writer, David Melnick, has put it) "re-claiming the American language from the trash heap." If the corporate world and the media have given us an objectionable jargon, what the language school has managed to do isn't to deconstruct that jargon, but to substitute another jargon for it—one that's every bit as impenetrable by common sense. Much of their new anthology's critical prose is written in it (see Steve Benson's essay "For Change," with its anti-"outsider" rhetoric and smug insistence on the mechanical competency of his friends' writing: "apparent units within their works often function by apparently nonprogrammatic and yet highly intentional juxtapositions . . . "). Unfortunately, the jargon also leaks over into the poetry, which comes out sounding a little like the drone of Hal the Computer in *2001.*

These writers have indeed, as Ron Silliman claims, rejected "speech" and thrown out the "speech-based" poetics of William Carlos Williams, but at what price? Williams's historic decision to base his writing on the spoken American language— paralleling Chaucer's decision to write in English instead of Latin or French, the "literary languages" of his time—was the great democratic gesture of poetry in this century, expanding its audience to fulfill the grandly inclusive aims of Walt Whitman. The language school has set out to draw back the perimeters of that audience, contracting poetry until it fits around only themselves.

Worlds of Up and Down

Thomas McGrath's *Letter to an Imaginary Friend: Parts Three &
Four* is the conclusion of a grand visionary poem whose first
two parts appeared in 1962 and 1970. It's a big (nearly 3,500
lines in this volume), risky work, defying the cautiously functional, Swedish-modern, small-is-beautiful tendencies of most
recent American poetry—and evoking instead such major,
mountain-range-size poems as *Leaves of Grass, The Cantos* and
Maximus. Not that McGrath imitates Whitman, Pound or Olson, all of whom he resembles more in his choice of a large
canvas than in what he covers it with.

At the age of seventy, McGrath is still the kind of writer
who takes chances on every page, sticking his neck out on the
premise that, while embarrassing yourself now and then
proves you're human ("so weak, so poor, in that cold wind"), it
also thereby qualifies you to "leap / into heaven"; without
doing one, you can't do the other, his work seems to say.

And, indeed, it's the tension between those two states that
drives this book: that is, between what McGrath calls "the
Horizontal, the World of Down"—that bleak existential plain,
wide and cold as a winter prairie, wherein we fallen mortals
toil—and what he terms "the World of Up, the Vertical," the
world of magic and spirits into which his autobiographical
boy-narrator ascends while dreaming in a Christmas sled. ("I
climb on the shivering ladder of Quaking Aspen boughs . . .")

McGrath's "World of Up" is a theological conception, evok-

Review of *Letter to an Imaginary Friend: Parts Three & Four* by Thomas
McGrath, *San Francisco Chronicle,* 1985.

ing a primal world of transcendence whose legacy to us is nature.

This poet has long made man's greedy arrogation of nature-as-property—the evil hunger for "power over the world" that turns it into " 'dead nature' . . . so and so many board feet and so much profit and loss"—the major villain of his work. Here he goes beyond simply decrying this greed and tries, in a poem he describes as a "revolutionary act," to supplant it with "a view which all primitives, anyone who has spent time in the woods or anyone simply in his/her right mind has always had: that Nature is just as alive as we are." (The quotes are from his preface.)

Of course this kind of "revolutionary" intention has inspired other poets before McGrath, most notably Wordsworth, who came back from a visit to the France of the Revolution with strange new ideas about the common life of nature in men and other forms of being. And Wordsworth's exploration of "the birth of the poet's mind" in *The Prelude* contains a template for many passages here.

One is McGrath's remarkable ice-skating sequence, so close to Wordsworth in its grasp of the relation between the life of nature and the life of the imagination:

> Under us a lattice, thin as a molecule, grows
> Instantaneous—formed (just under our feet as we flash
> Forward over our world) like the forming of winter ice
> Over the river . . .
>   and we skate onward carolling:
> "Over the ice!"
> Never aware how thin
> That winter ice is . . . formed for an instant under our feet
> Then vanishing . . .
> Or in summer as waterwalkers we skate
> The dogday rivers . . .
>   the thin skin of the water holding
> An instant that is ours forever as we rush out to the stars.

The dramatic center of *Parts Three & Four*—a work that swings off into symbolic sub-orbits of Hopi mythology and medieval occultism before it's over—is a Christmas Eve and morning in a North Dakota frontier hamlet sometime in the early 1920s. In his narrative passages on the preparations for Midnight Mass, the feast that follows and the sleigh ride home, we encounter that theological legacy of McGrath's at its most intense. He contacts the ancient experiences beneath the Christian rituals, reconstituting the icy awe and wonder of a long festive night—as filtered through the sensitized soul of a ten-year-old.

Memory is a dominant theme of McGrath's poem. He is obsessed with the uniqueness of event, the sadness that each thing happens once and no more (making past experiences into so many turned-over "pages" in an endless book). What makes all these particular losses bearable, the poet seems to say, is their participation in greater chords of meaning that span decades and centuries.

Those chords, in fact, are his specialty. He finds natural metaphor everywhere—instances of a pulsing, difference-denying "life in nature" that carry out the plan of his poem, making it into vigorous actuality. The stars above his snow-bound Dakota prairie don't just hang there, they "reel" and "rush" and "dance." The Northern Lights don't only shine, they "string a harp toward the far pole": a rooster doesn't merely crow, it "prays for sunrise / Like a muezzin left in the rain so long that his voice is rusty."

The best test of how much light a poet is directing in his poems is whether the beam of his attention on his chosen subject also illuminates things around it, crystalizing and giving shape to a whole field of objects, making them glow with shared clarity. In opening up one cell of reality, the poet's attention spills over and penetrates the next. This process of overflowing operates all through McGrath's long poem.

Northern Connection

Sister Goodwin lives in Sitka, Alaska, and was born above the Arctic Circle. Her *A Lagoon Is in My Backyard* comes advertised as the "first book ever published by an Eskimo female writer in history." While that's noteworthy enough, what makes Sister Goodwin's poems interesting isn't anything as simple as ethnics or gender.

She writes about her native North with a quick sense of elemental metaphor and natural process, apprehending force fields that congregate in language when high energy currents of timeless collective myth and present-tense personal history intersect.

These poems occur in a medium of transformation. Under the enveloping luminosity of Goodwin's polar lights, "a soft glow of ions" clings to human forms, attention is supercharged, and perceptual changes take place as naturally as—we might say—walking across the street on a sunny day; except that here the street's an ice pack or snow bluff, and the temperature is "thirty below zero"—like "feeling thirty hard-packed snowballs / hit you in the face all at once."

The sense of communal function in these poems is strong. Goodwin writes not in the tone of an originator but of one extending the messages of ancestors who "took me back / to when time was cast." The process of acculturation of Eskimo tribes into Americanized contemporary society is viewed by Goodwin as a sad one. Her finest poem, "families tied," ad-

---

Review of *A Lagoon Is in My Backyard* by Sister Goodwin, *San Francisco Chronicle*, 1985.

dresses this subject with the kind of argument-by-understatement that only the best poetry can make.

She begins the poem by invoking her "great great grandparents," who "knew only inupiaq ways"—including the custom by which "two men exchanged camps / lived with each other's woman / and fathered each other's children." When such children grew up, they felt "pride / to be / the connection / to another family / in another village"; "transposition / made the families conjugal." Then, however,

> strange new men came and told the inupiaq
> it was a life of heathens
> immoral
> deplorable
> you primitives
> belong in the Pleistocene
> back with the Neanderthal
> and now inupiat sleep
> with each other
> to connect
> only themselves.

However sad the changes in Eskimo life wrought by Americanization, sadder still are the Americans who've come to Alaska expecting the "conveniences" they left behind. Like the "bump on a log" Goodwin encounters in her poem "beachcombing"—"who started the / campfire conversation / by announcing he / comes from wisconsin / or maybe he said / tillamook / he's way up here / wondering how / to get pasteurized milk."

He won't find anything pasteurized in Sister Goodwin's poems.

Aerial Spaces and
Reverberating Depths

A winner of this year's American Book Awards (The Before Columbus Foundation), *Amelia Earhart* is a kind of freestyle lyric verse biography of the pioneering woman aviator. It is also a celebration of air, space and American plains geography; and a breezily eccentric, stereotype-busting tribute to the perennial irrepressibility and daring of the woman-spirit.

Maureen Owen's Earhart is half historical figure, half imaginative creation. Owen's view of the exuberant, cocky, irreverent, surprising tomboy-flier is decidedly personal; it's also disconcertingly contemporary. Her story makes gulping time-leaps, often into the present moment: Her narrator and Earhart smoke pot "under the fuselage," discuss space shuttles and nuclear weapons, dunk Oreos in coffee and make love in the hangar, "hugging & sloshing in spilled motor oil."

The poet-as-narrator shares with her aviator subject a love of open spaces. "AE" is a poem "about space & claustrophobia," Owen announces. Earhart's Kansas sense of the generosity of plains spaces echoes the narrator's own experience of huge Minnesota horizons: "O geography My Great Flat Home." The bountiful wheat fields of the Midwest ("land & air / Unrolled" over "acre upon acre") are Owen's image of an earthbound expansiveness to match Earhart's discoveries

---

Review of *Amelia Earhart* by Maureen Owen and *Where the Island Sleeps Like a Wing* by Nancy Morejon, translated by Kathleen Weaver, *San Francisco Chronicle,* 1985.

of the spatial bounties of the sky and her defiance of the confinement of the cockpit, the "morbid dread of closure—physical and social."

Images of opening and expansion are the heart of the poem. "There's this weight on my chest & now it's just / Gone completely gone. I'm airy as feathers / half the world is sky it's just everywhere you / won't see sky like that except out there."

"Out there" in the free dimensions of legend, Earhart hovers as the perfect poetic Muse (inspirer, breath-giver) over this poem whose honest diction she also endows ("I don't know about no 'Muse' ") with an earthiness of real spoken language.

Owen's Earhart takes off into a lyrical wild blue yonder with that kind of buoyant, soaring adventurousness that has won women greater freedom in current times. Earhart is both a real figure here and the flexible emblem of an ideal.

> People like us want it back she
>   tells me
> We want to flatten everything around us Always
>   Clearing
> Clearing Pushing   making space We want acre upon
> acre upon acre the plains . . . the
>   flat runway before us
> the song of the engine the terrible velocity &
>   then
> the space it's the moment inbetween the thing
> at the end of it all what we are always after that
>   Flat
> that lucid that unstopped Opening! the Space . .

Amelia Earhart defies gravity, leaping from terra firma to new aerial spaces. Nancy Morejon's *Where the Island Sleeps Like a Wing*, on the other hand, drops to earth from tropic night skies like an unexpected, elemental gift—an "obsidian meteorite," as her fellow Cuban poet Miguel Barnet says in his introduction to this first American selection of her work, very ably put into English by Berkeley translator Kathleen Weaver.

Morejon's deceptively simple, limpid lines start at the surface and sink very deep, like plummets gauging the reverberating depths of a spiritual life beyond the range of most contemporary poets.

A black Cuban, Morejon writes of her island with a Latin / African intensity and heat, capturing in vivid images its sea foam, sugary flowers, perfumed breezes—the natural lan guage of a Caribbean air dense with "aromas and orange trees." It's no easy postcard descriptiveness, this language, but a native sediment of the heart, leached from generations of pain. "I still smell the foam of the sea they made me cross . . . They left me here and here I've lived," Morejon writes in "Black Woman." "This is the land where I suffered / mouth-in-the-dust and the lash . . . I sang to the beat of pure native birds . . . I touched the fresh blood and decayed bones of many others."

Alice Walker has expressed the delight of recognizing in Morejon's work the sound of "a black woman who is at peace with her country." This tone of acceptance is real, and hard-won—the product of long historical struggle.

> From the sixteenth century dates my suffering
> though I barely felt it
> for that nightingale
> always sings in my suffering.
>
> ("Looking Within")

History is regarded by many poets as an annoying distraction. To Morejon it's a powerful poetic source. Her heroines are as real as Amelia Earhart, but instead of pioneer Yankee air-athletes they're Third World warrior-women, like Angela Davis or Cheng Tseh and Cheng Urh, the horseback lady generals of Vietnamese history.

She writes about the Bay of Pigs and the Battle of Teruel, celebrates nationally famous heroes of the Cuban revolution like Abel Santamaria and Camilo Cienfuegos, and promotes poetically the worldwide struggle for independence of people of color, from Kingstontown to Oakland—where she addresses an apple tree that's "been / the sad, cruel, shadowy, the ephemeral dwelling / of multitudinous black heads hanging among the foliage, incorruptible."

Her poetry is political in the best sense; it shares and makes particular the sufferings of the underprivileged and repressed. Bad political poetry is a sad beast of burden, bowed under the weight of concept. Nancy Morejon's poems are pre-conceptual; they present an image of human dignity that transcends the pain of the condition of being human:

> Sullen and serene,
> without the deceitful braid,
> in embalmed silence,
> you watch
> the step of death approach.
>
> Your set mouth,
> pausing like a great bird
> over the plain, speaks:
> *Death is the best misfortune,*
> *because it wipes out all others.*
> ("Tata on the Death of Don Pablo")

At her best—in pieces like "Solaris," "Your Law" and "The Sleep of Reason Produces Monsters"—Morejon's writing has the metaphysical tension only great poetry can attain. Such lines as "Floating weightless, dead algae for radar, / I arrived at love" ("Solaris") sound this metaphysical note. It's sometimes present in whole passages, like this from the complex "Your Law":

> Your mind will be free
> of all dryness. A noble parade
> will open in your memory.
> You wake up.
> The concentration camp
> is an incurable madman
> howling in sterility.
> Oh pure friend of triumphant Chile,
> this white page shivers with your fever,
> it waits the passage of the nightmare

that will flee like a rabbit, punished
by the law of the strongest,
which is your law.
That will be the instant of splendor.

A Good House

When Kenneth Rexroth hit town in 1927, San Francisco was strictly a nothing burg, culturally speaking—at least in the eyes of this twenty-two-year-old whirlwind. "Very much of a backwater town," Rexroth later described it, "there just wasn't anything happening."

The cultural vacuum by the Bay couldn't withstand Rexroth for long. He wrote poems (*In What Hour*, 1940), edited a mimeograph weekly to organize dockworkers (*Waterfront Worker*), promoted anarchism and radicalism over the radio, shot from the hip as a reviewer for the *Chronicle*, sponsored the Beats, emceed the debut performance of *Howl* at the Six Gallery and—to hear him tell it—hatched the San Francisco Renaissance practically single-handedly.

All this is obvious history, and well known. What it tends to obscure is the poetry that was Rexroth's great gift, and which his recent death leaves us with, now that the poet and the voice are gone.

Even now, two years after his death, it's hard to believe Rexroth's no longer around. A spirit as flinty and tenacious as the Sierra granites that towered over the campsites where he composed many of his poems, Rexroth always seemed to be one writer who might just go on forever. Certainly his work promoted the impression. The wayward or cantankerous moments in his critical writing—as opinionated, articulate and interesting as that always was—never struck one as being so

Review of *The Selected Poems of Kenneth Rexroth*, edited by Bradford Morrow, *San Francisco Chronicle*, 1985.

characteristic of the man as those very different moments of ecstatic revelation, the still points at the center of his finest poems, where the reader is invited into an impersonal understanding of life and nature that is literally timeless.

Rexroth's best poems take place in the High Sierra, far from human noise, under the whirling oceans of stars, among peaks and waterfalls and streams, in clearings surrounded by the night eyes of raccoons, the hoofprints of deer in snow. These contemplative lyrics achieve a sense of mystical solitude, natural awe and wonder that recalls the Greek, Chinese and Japanese classics which were Rexroth's models.

In his poems Rexroth set out to achieve a reductionist simplicity—what he called "fidelity to objectively verifiable experience"—but ended up getting all his best effects by leaping outside and beyond those experiential bits and pieces into the same emotional, moral and spiritual realms where great poetry has always taken us. Endlessly eclectic, he was also a traditionalist in the best sense, taking from past literature those things that he could use—simplicity, clarity and depth.

Poised statement and simple, clear image were his only tools as a poet. He had little gift for metaphor and as a result largely disdained it. His fellow poet William Carlos Williams, who wrote one of the best assessments of Rexroth's work, pointed out that "he is no writer in the sense of a word-man. For him words are sticks and stones to build a house—but it's a good house."

It's a house that has held up well over the years. The nature poems, and to a lesser extent the love poems (which are really a subdivision of the former genre, since in Rexroth's work sexual love is something that usually occurs in *plein air* settings, as a continuity of landscape), provide the foundation. Along with Robinson Jeffers's, Rexroth's work introduced to our literature the very special character of West Coast landscape, its way of dwarfing and diminishing the encroaching human element—which had never before looked so tiny and temporary as when seen up against this colossal backdrop of mountain and sea. Out of the common Jeffers-Rexroth seed has grown the very vigorous tradition of West Coast nature poetry, still extending in the work of such writers as William Everson and Gary Snyder.

Few poets have no failings. Rexroth's bad moments occur when his poems turn into prose tracts aimed at cardboard opponents. He had a dowser's instinct for detecting the dark side of human nature. William Carlos Williams called him "a moralist with his hand at the trigger ready to fire at the turn of a hair." Rexroth's articulated moral rages often proved fascinating in his occasional essays, but in the poetry there's a silly ring to many of his pronunciamentos. My favorite silly Rexroth pronouncement: "You will find . . . more love, in an hour / In the arms of a pickup in / Singapore or Reykjavik, / Than you will in a lifetime / Married to a middle class / White American woman."

Kenneth Rexroth was perhaps the original West Coast hipster. He spent a lot of his time baiting the squares. (Kenneth was so hip, to him even Jack Kerouac was a square.) His political poetry suffers seriously from square-phobia, particularly the memorial elegy for Dylan Thomas, "Thou Shalt Not Kill," which blames Thomas's demise on suburbanite-corporate types in "Brooks Brothers suits."

Urban Pastoral

As Robert Creeley points out in his introduction to *Collected Poems,* William Corbett is a poet of city nature. He trains the strict and patient attention of a rural realist on the seldom noticed pastoral attraction of the urban scene.

"I spent the spring walking around Boston," Corbett writes. "Two 95 / degree days like a trick / lengthened Boylston Street. Spring / . . . came overnight, and you could / not see across the Public Garden / by morning." Corbett's ecstatic catalog of the sudden, visibility-obscuring abundance of May blossoms shows his urban pastoralist's eye: "lilac more grape than lavender," "horse chestnut seeds / like creme horns drifting," "wisteria hung glamorously / from an alley fence," "soft dogwood / petals in the grass," and finally the climactic "magnolia burst / pink and white then gone" ("Runaway Pond").

In March, Corbett writes of the city's first slowly unfurling irises—"Spring now / here not just yet / but robins on the feeble / green dirty winter strewn grass / squirrels yes and pigeons / sheets on the line / crisp March / crocus breaking through / the low sun blinding / smeared and dusty window / tongues of egg yellow / these purply blue and / white arching flowers / on tall stalks like torches" ("A Torn Page").

The urban pastoral is a mode that doesn't try to overpower. It sneaks up on you, woos, wins you over gently and a little at a time.

Corbett's poetry is in no hurry, it inches along at a snail's

Review of *Collected Poems* by William Corbett, *San Francisco Chronicle,* 1985.

pace of close attention—"to be slow to be whole." At first glance these quiet, diaristic inventory poems look like indiscriminate records of the chance track of daily experience. And some of them—"Columbus Square Journal," a year's poem-commonplace-book—are obviously meant to work as such. They allow a nice casual access to all kinds of material. Another way of putting it is that they're like flypaper; a lot of domestic dailiness sticks to them.

When Corbett writes, as he so often does, about fruit—the "jolly comice pear" wobbling on the table, the "sweet pale orange flesh" of the Cranshaw melon, the "color of frost on apples," "peaches in the bowl ripening," etc.—I'm reminded of William Carlos Williams's classic American urban pastoral image, the plums in the icebox. Like Williams, Philip Whalen, James Schuyler, Frank O'Hara and other flypaper poets—all masters of the urban pastoral, too, and big influences on his own work—Corbett labors to capture not only a cool picture of casual experience, but its peculiar personal flavor. His details accumulate to state a life.

Corbett's conversational tone turns reflective and elegiac as the forest of daily events turns deep and dark. The burden of his melancholy is the past: "I carry the past like a mailman letters." He suffers from the urban man's chronic pessimism, bred of obsession with time—"as if a sure future / could order a difficult present." The oppression of time and mortality is relieved in Corbett's poems by the proximity of a pastoral space—even if it's only his stamp-sized piece of garden, or some metropolitan skaters' thin ribbon of ice. He rambles through in an agreeable discursive voice, with its ring of a New England Wordsworth gone to seed on the South Common, ear tuned to the Aeolian harp of a Red Sox broadcast.

It's a voice that's easy to trust, nowhere more than in the ruminative, layered narrative of longer pieces like "Runaway Pond" and "February 29th." Here William Corbett does his best writing in a kind of post-Williams blank verse that transfigures the past and "thoughts of death / and dying," submerging both in an "otherworld / underworld" from which spring's first blooms spire upwards like "open / orange trumpets."

These works show how the relation of the patient eye to the transitory beauties of the city can revive the urban pastoral in any age. You can't put these poems into flowerpots, but they do brighten the day.

Digging into the Past

At age forty-five, Seamus Heaney is justly acknowledged as Ireland's finest living poet, and perhaps its best since Yeats. In *Station Island*—his eighth volume of verse in twenty years—he expands and amplifies that reputation. Rooted in the rugged ground of the local and physical, Heaney's work also extends vertical shafts into his country's history and mythology, tapping its rich and tragic past.

His own metaphor in this book for this act of discovery is that of a ball of twine unraveling, revealing successive segments of the past: "So the twine unwinds and loosely widens / backward through areas that forwarded / understandings of all I would undertake." While those lines are voiced for Sweeney, a seventh-century king of Ulster whose persona dominates the last of the book's three sections, they speak equally for the poet himself, unraveling the complex coils of personal and national identity.

Heaney is amply possessed with the Irish gift for sensuous and lyrical speech, but the bass note that drives his writing, that gives it impulsion, solidity and coherence, is simple, basic, monosyllabic Anglo-Saxon English.

That has always been his strength and it explains why he's always written so well about hard work. Heaney knows how to charge words with the weight and drag of physical labor. Finding a rusted railroad spike in a ditch summons to his mind an image of the long-gone sledge-wielder's "sweat-cured haft." Another poem evokes laborers observed in childhood—the

---

Review of *Station Island* by Seamus Heaney, *San Francisco Chronicle*, 1985.

bricklayer's "trowel dressing a brickbat" ("the tock and tap of its butt"), the sandpit-digger's "heft and lift" of a shovel, and the way "a tremor blunts the shaft / at small come-uppances meeting / the driven edge." Elsewhere he recalls the "brutal pull and drive" of an Irish ploughman, and his mother's "dumb lunge" over a smoothing iron.

These poems are hard to follow without a quick sense of the "jaggy, salty, punitive" granites of English roots: Heaney sent me back to the OED for *scrabs, dulse, slub, morse, scutch, stooked, flensed, mirled.*

Words are Heaney's medium as completely as a tool in the hands of an experienced workman—or flesh under the hand of a lover. He writes of an adolescent's "nightly shadow feasts / Haunting the granaries of words like *breasts*," of being "invited by the brush of a word like *peignoir.*" Visiting Thomas Hardy's birthplace, Heaney speaks of that writer's "words coming to rest: *birthplace, roofbeam, whitewash, / flagstone, hearth,* / like un-stacked iron weights afloat among galaxies."

The core of this book is the ambitious twelve-part title sequence, which engages Heaney's past—and Ireland's—in a method adapted from Dante. Set on Station Island in Lough Derg, County Donegal, a traditional pilgrimage site established by St. Patrick, the poem is cast in the Dantesque form of a dream journey into the world of the dead.

On the course of his journey the poet-pilgrim meets up with familiar ghosts—poets, teachers, friends—who teach him to recognize he has "somehow broken / covenants, and failed an obligation." Forced to reassess and "repent" an "unweaned life," he learns in a climactic encounter with the ghost of James Joyce to "swim out," into his "own element," away from both his own former weakness and from Ireland's historical cycle of tragedy and conflict. The poem ends in a "Paradiso"-like moment, among flashes and "elver-gleams." "It was as if I had stepped free into space."

Of course, Dante is a pretty elevated model to live up to. Heaney's long poem has flat stretches where inspiration lags and the bones of the program stick out through the verse that clothes it. But even though it doesn't have the metaphysical dimensions of Dante, it does succeed in accounting, through dramatic narrative, for "the growth of the poet's mind," à la Wordsworth's *Prelude*. And one section, at least, ranks with the most powerful visionary poems in the language—Part VII, wherein a friend killed in political troubles returns with a bullet hole in his head, impacting the poet with realization of his own "indifference" and "circumspect involvement."

The metaphor of memory or vision as a journey to the underworld appears not only in the title sequence, "Station Island," but in the book's opening piece, one of Heaney's finest short lyrics. Both poems pivot on the same irony: rediscovering an image out of the past only underscores its fatal loss. In "The Underground," however, Heaney turns not to Dante's Christian myth for structure but to a prior legend, the tale of Orpheus and Eurydice:

> There we were in the vaulted tunnel running,
> You in your going-away coat speeding ahead
> And me, me then like a fleet god gaining
> Upon you before you turned into a reed
>
> Or some new white flower japped with crimson
> As the coat flapped wild and button after button
> Sprang off and fell in a trail
> Between the Underground and the Albert Hall.
>
> Honeymooning, moonlighting, late for the Proms,
> Our echoes die in that corridor and now
> I come as Hansel came on the moonlit stones
> Retracing the path back, lifting the buttons.
>
> To end up in a draughty lamplit station
> After the trains have gone, the wet track
> Bared and tensed as I am, all attention
> For your step following and damned if I look back.

From Loch Ness to Ruskin

Picking up the two-volume *Complete Poems* of prolific Scots bard Hugh MacDiarmid isn't easy. There are 1,494 pages of fine print in these chunky volumes that, stacked together, probably weigh five pounds.

MacDiarmid's work is even more abundant in spirit than in physical bulk. Sometimes an amazing blowhard, spouting long tracts of political, aesthetic and philosophical doggerel, much of whose polymathic "learning" comes off sounding as eccentric as a Loch Ness monster playing the bagpipes, this poet is also capable of pulling off a brief lyric that cancels all the surrounding excesses by springing the secrets of life and death on you:

> Stop killin' the deid. Gi'e owre
> Your weepin' and wailin'.
> You maun keep quiet
> If you want to hear them still
> And no' blur their image in your mind.
>
> For they've only a faint wee whisperin' voice
> Makin' nae mair noise ava'
> Than the growin' o' the grass
> That flourishes whaur naebody walks.
> ("Weep and Wail No More")

A lot of great lyricists die young. Hugh MacDiarmid (born Christopher Murray Grieve, 1892) had the staying power of a

Review of *The Complete Poems* by Hugh MacDiarmid and *Selected Poems* by Donald Davie, *San Francisco Chronicle,* 1985.

draft horse. He lived nearly into his nineties, and in his eighties was still writing lines like those above from 1970.

But his finest work can be found in two books of haunting Scots lyrics published five-and-a-half decades earlier, *Penny Wheep* (1926) and *Sangschaw* (1925), when MacDiarmid's revival of the language of Robert Burns first saw the light in poems like "The Eemis Stane":

> I' the how-dumb-deid o' the cauld hairst nicht
> The warl' like an eemis stane
> Wags i' the lift;
> An' my eerie memories fa'
> Like a yowdendrift.

Perhaps the classic metaphysical compression of MacDiarmid's Scots lyrics is best indicated by how many more words it takes to get them across in English—in this case something like: "In the dead middle of the cold harvest night / The world like a thrown stone wobbling in its trajectory / Wags in the sky / And my eerie memories fall / Like a snow-whirl countering earth-drift."

A convinced Communist and modernist of a decidedly international persuasion, MacDiarmid wrote not only in his idiosyncratic mixture of archaic literary Scots and contemporary Scottish vernacular but in English, which he used for his long-winded verse sermons and some shorter poems. The political writing in English is at times of interest for the vituperative razor-thrust of its hatred, its wicked wry humor or for the rousing organ-music of emotional conviction.

By and large, however, MacDiarmid's poems in English are hard slogging. Most of them are long—very. He is even more inclusive than Whitman, if that can be believed.

If the long English poems now provoke yawns, the shorter ones in Scottish are still capable of inducing awe, wonder—and an occasional laugh, as in his many lines on the subject of his love/hate relation with his native country.

British poet Donald Davie's *Selected Poems* collects work from fifteen prior volumes dating back to the 1950s. Davie's poetry is quiet, reflective, learned and consistently decorous, even at its most personal. He calls himself, accurately and only half-ironically, a "neo-classicist"; his close attention to history and quick sense of personal ethics combine to make him also a pessimist about human nature, despite his commitment to the aesthetic principles of humanism.

Davie has ranged abroad, both in person (visiting Italy and France, teaching in America at Stanford and Vanderbilt) and in preoccupation. (His poems and criticism show a very un-British susceptibility to foreign influence, from Pushkin to Pasternak, Pound to Edward Dorn.) But for all the exotic input, Davie's Wesleyan-conservative upbringing shows through with bony persistence in all his writing.

In the poems this natural conservatism juts out like an exposed nerve, exhibiting a raw and smarting sensitivity to the specious, the affected or the merely easy: "I cannot abide the new / Absurdities day by day, / The new adulterations . . ." ("Epistle to Enrique Caracciolo Trejo"). "My strongest feeling all / My life has been, / I recognize, revulsion / From the obscene . . . / That so much more reaction / Than action should have swayed / My life and rhymes / Must be the heaviest charge / That can be brought against / Me, or my times" ("Revulsion").

The critic in Davie is no less a self-critic. He often upbraids himself for a characteristically English deficiency of emotion in his life—and in his poems. The problem, he suggests at one point, is language itself—the poor-spirited, narrow, "constricted idiom" of English in which he's both writing and feeling. "The English that I feel in / Fears the inauthentic / Which invades it on all sides / Mortally" ("Epistle"). The basis for this constriction, Davie proposes, is a general "humiliation, corporate and private" which has slowly gained a stranglehold over the whole of British culture.

"Constricted" or not, he soldiers on in his given idiom—manipulating it very skillfully in careful, argumentative poems whose pristine diction, suspensefully unfolding syntax and precise attentions capture—like much of the best reflective writing in English—the pleasures, however modest, of truth. Something akin to Hardy's sense of "thwarted purposings" is there in Davie, as is a clarity and sharpness of aesthetic response similar to Ruskin's:

> Twigs crack under foot, as the tread
> Changes. The forge-ahead style
> Of our earliest ventures flags;
> It becomes, as mile follows mile
> Inexhaustibly, an exhausted
> Wavering trudge, the explorer's.
>
> ("Oak Openings")

Poetry of Exile

Some may argue that a writer is a self-exile by definition, that to write is to turn away from the world. But speaking practically as well, in this century it has been common for writers to find themselves far from home. With some, it has happened voluntarily—Joyce, Pound, Stein. Others have been forced into exile for political reasons: One thinks of Mann and Brecht in Hollywood, Malaparte in Capri, Céline in Denmark, Solzhenitzyn in Siberia. Whatever the conditions of internment, whether a California beach house, a polar gulag, a Baltic cabin—or, in the case of Greek poet Yannis Ritsos, an island in the Aegean—all such writers report experiencing to some degree or other the peculiar chill of exile.

Ritsos's stark, haunting *Exile and Return: Selected Poems 1967–1974* is classic poetry of exile.

This is writing inhabited by feelings of apprehension, dread and loss. In verse as stripped and final as an obituary, Ritsos's poems transmit images of dislocation and alienation similar to those encountered in the distorted spaces of nightmare: empty, washed-out sunshine, echoing silence, looming, half-sentient statues looking on like enigmatic sentinels over arid, eerie landscapes of absence reminiscent of the early canvases of Ritsos's countryman, Giorgio de Chirico. Inside the houses, people in masks, in front of mirrors, aging slowly, crippled, mute or blind, reflect on the myths of the past,

Review of *Exile and Return: Selected Poems 1967–1974* by Yannis Ritsos, translated by Edmund Keeley, and *The Granite Pail: Selected Poems* by Lorine Niedecker, edited by Cid Corman, *San Francisco Chronicle*, 1985.

propitiate the many dead and prepare for worse horrors yet to come.

A Greek Communist and alleged "dissenter," Ritsos was arrested after the right-wing coup of 1967 and held by the government—first in prison camps on various Greek islands, then later in exile and under house arrest on the island of Samos. Finally, he returned to his Athens apartment where he lived in seclusion and self-exile during the last few years of the military dictatorship.

These poems record the repression and terror of the period. They also capture a very modern sense of exile not only from place but from shared values. The crumbling statuary and broken rituals that occupy Ritsos so obsessively are objectifications of the death of both the Hellenistic mythological world and the Christian tradition that followed it. What remains here is uneasy mystery, confusion and ruins all around. This book could be taken as a poetic chronicle, catching the last ripple in time of a civilization submerged not merely by external violence but by the tacit agreement of its citizens— whom Ritsos holds responsible for their collective downfall, if only by what he calls (in the title of one poem) "Guilt by Abstention."

> We couldn't stand what was empty, uninhabited. Often we
>   would move
> the huge mirror to the river bank, a chair
> into a tree, and at other times, conversely,
> a huge tree into the dining room. Then we would hear
> the gunfire behind the sheepfold, late, at dusk,
> and though known and expected, it would always startle us—
> this our confirmation for the proper placing of words.
>   ("Enlightenment")

Historically, professional literature has been largely a male province. Until recently, if you were someone with a calling to write, having been born a woman was itself a form of exile. Like Emily Dickinson, Lorine Niedecker (*The Granite Pail: Selected Poems*) was a great poet who was virtually unknown by the American reading public during her lifetime.

When she married, late in life, Niedecker carefully refrained from informing her husband that she wrote poems until after the wedding. Later, when he revealed the secret to friends, she grew embarrassed and upbraided him for it. She never read her poems in public and refused even to be tape-recorded. A poet who visited her remarked that she seemed "lonely, eager for intellectual company but unable to foment it, fearful of the 'larger' scene."

Her poetry shares with Dickinson's not only the reflective lyric form but a quality that Niedecker once described in a letter as "depth of emotion condensed . . . a kind of shine (or somber tone) that is of the same intensity throughout the poem."

Niedecker was born in Wisconsin just after the turn of this century and raised in the green, wet Rock River marshland country around Fort Atkinson where her father was a carp fisherman and tavern keeper; after his death she cared for her invalid mother. At the age of eighteen, in 1921, she bought a book of Wordsworth's poems and soon afterward began writing poems of her own. "Grandfather / advised me," she writes in one poem, "learn a trade. I learned / to sit at desk / and condense. / No layoff / from this / condensery" ("Poet's Work").

Niedecker herself worked in a bank, the local library and a print shop, then later scrubbed floors in the hospital. At the age of sixty she retired and married a very non-literary, one-armed Minnesota backwoodsman who'd once ridden the rails out West. They divided the last seven years of her life between Milwaukee, where he was a building painter, and her beloved Fort Atkinson with its floods and trees that she memorialized in her poems—often composed while her husband watched football games on television.

The poems are mostly very short. Niedecker insisted that poets ought to consider silence an ally—"and the great, ever present possibility that our poems may not get read." As if modestly aware of taking up too much of her busy readers' time, she gave over only her essential vision; her work contains almost no marginalia.

Though in her middle life the poems began to appear in the extremely small circulation of little magazines and overseas small press editions, it was not until after her death that they started to gather the recognition they deserve. Niedecker is now acknowledged widely for the formalist pleasures of her work, which have caused critics to place her retroactively alongside "objectivist" masters like Louis Zukofsky and Charles Reznikoff. But equally compelling is its "shine" of intensity as human information—including her reflections on a personal struggle with the loss and waste imposed on women artists by the culture: "I've wasted my whole life in water," Niedecker writes typically. "Think what's got away in my life . . ." "There's a better shine / on the pendulum / than is on my hair / and many times / I've seen it there."

Grounding Transcendence

The Sonnets to Orpheus was composed, according to Rainer Maria Rilke, all in one unrevised burst in a few weeks of February, 1922. From his endless letters to countesses and baronesses about the circumstances of composition, we know that this must have been an extraordinary outburst of inspiration.

Rilke's own voluminous testimony on the subject is provided (along with some out-of-sequence sonnets and fragments never before put into English) in Stephen Mitchell's notes, appended to his translation of the *Sonnets*. "On February 2," Mitchell writes in his introduction, Rilke "disappeared into the god . . . When life occurs at this level of intensity, biography turns into myth. The myth here resembles that of Psyche and Eros . . . the god enters, she is caught up in a fulfillment beyond her most extravagant hope."

Divinely inspired or not, these poems present special difficulties for the translator. First, there are the problems of German itself—"that floundering language," D. H. Lawrence called it, "a beastly language, one that doesn't fit the cells of the brain." Rilke's sonnets, moreover, contain curious grammatical impulses and metaphorical ambiguities that make literal translation very difficult—and reading such translations even more so. What's merely opaque in German often comes off sounding pompous, affected or vaguely silly in English.

The closest thing to a literal rendering of *The Sonnets to Orpheus* is the 1942 version by M. D. Herter Norton. The present contender, Stephen Mitchell (whose *Selected Poetry of*

Review of *The Sonnets to Orpheus* by Rainer Maria Rilke, translated by Stephen Mitchell, *San Francisco Chronicle,* 1985.

Rilke deserved all the praise it got when it appeared a few years back) tends to follow the discerning Norton on word choices, if not on syntax. But like C. F. MacIntyre (whose translation came out in 1960), Mitchell is at the same time intolerant of Rilke's ambiguities; he takes liberties. Where MacIntyre's presumptions led him into some non-sequitur absurdities, however, Mitchell sticks to clear English.

At its best, Rilke's poetry is formal, powerful, fast and fluent, with an insistent rhetoric of transformation and transcendence that's one of its trademarks. Other characteristics are a grand music, an expressive syntax, a dominant symbolic use of nouns, a general tone of prophetic invocation mixed with premonitions of religiosity and traces of a romantic longing for the infinite that's rather anachronistic in a "modern."

And it's this last quality—the religious, essentialist Rilke, full of manipulations of illusions, voids and scintillating microreflections of vast cosmic spaces—that Stephen Mitchell seems to apprehend best:

> Silent friend of many distances, feel
> how your breath enlarges all of space.
> Let your presence ring out like a bell into the night . . .
> And if the earthly no longer knows your name,
> whisper to the silent earth: I'm flowing.
> To the flashing water say: I am.

Compare Norton: "Silent friend of many distances, / feel how your breath is still increasing space. / Among the beams of the dark belfries let / yourself ring out . . . And if the earthly has forgotten you, / say to the still earth: I flow. / To the rapid water speak: I am."

And MacIntyre: "Still friend of many distances, feel yet / how your breathing is augmenting space. From the beamwork of gloomy belfries let / yourself ring . . . Though / earth itself forgot your very name, / say unto the tranquil earth: I flow. / To the fleeting water speak: I am."

Mitchell throws out the belfry, makes his "space" into that of night, has his poet "whisper" instead of "say," and finds "flashing" in the German *raschen*. The changes make all the difference, turning the English version from a stilted approximation of difficult German into a new order of creation.

There are, one hastens to say, passages where not even Stephen Mitchell can save Rilke from himself. Nostalgias of the most cloying kind are always lurking around the fringe of Rilke's work—a suspicion of the phony refinement of "art-for-art's-sake." This is the poet known for his ecstatic response to the smell of an old chest. Such manifestations are bound to leave any translator at a loss. Take Mitchell's unsuccessful struggle with these lines: "Look at the fish, served upon the gaily set table: / how peculiar its face on the dish." *You* look at it, I want to say.

But in Mitchell's translation of the *Sonnets,* the work's qualities outweigh its defects. The poems' difficult syntax and contorted phrasing are largely dispelled (along with Rilke's music, which simply can't be caught in English). The result is a fine set of English poems that catch very adeptly the heroic aspect of the German writer's poetic pursuit of transcendence.

The Sonnets to Orpheus are a triumph of the symbolist vision, "vague as the air and soluble, / with nothing heavy and at rest"—to quote Paul Verlaine's "*Art poetique,*" the Bible of Symbolism that ruled over Rilke's aesthetics. Mitchell has given the poems substance, contour and weight. They're now at rest in the earthy medium of English.

Snowfall inside a Paperweight

The Migration of Powers is the final volume in Graywolf's four-part series of translations of Rainer Maria Rilke's French poems. Now that this poet's German works are so widely read in English versions, the accomplished Rilke translator A. Poulin, Jr. has brought over most of the nearly 400 poems the poet wrote in French.

As Poulin himself admitted in the introduction to a previous volume of the series, Rilke's French poems offer no vast wrestlings with the gods, the angels or the dead. They do not "undertake great subjects and themes," but are rather "small poems of careful attentiveness to the things of this world, and to the elusive states of being in which the world is poetically transformed."

The combination of French and Rilke is like a marriage of cousins. French lends itself to abstraction, and Rilke's poetry naturally tends that way. Together the German poet and his adopted tongue produced poems at times cloudy, vague and soft, at other moments light, buoyant and graceful—full of "sighs" and "tender carelessness," like the "Soap Bubbles" of the poem so titled ("fabricating these round fruits / of nothingness"). The emotions they project are less urgent than idle, often retrospective and nostalgic, at once intimate and distant, almost always calm and serene—like "the calm of animals for whom anxiety / never insists / (as it does in us) on making them / habitually unhappy."

There are points in these poems where the sudden flashing-

Review of *The Migration of Powers* by Rainer Maria Rilke, translated by A. Poulin, Jr., *San Francisco Chronicle*, 1985.

out of mystical, prophetic metaphor, or the brooding absorption with death and spirituality, remind us that a powerful and familiar poetic imagination is at work. "Does the weight / of the dead add itself to the earth / to stop her cold?" ("The Heavy Dead"). "Future, who won't wait for you? / Everyone's going there. / It suffices you to deepen / the absence that we are" ("The Future").

But the general impression is of a milky abstractness. Reading Rilke's French in English, even in these very ably rendered versions, is like watching a snowfall inside a paperweight, or maybe the snow that fills a TV screen after the picture goes off at night. The "slow caress of shadows" and "stirring absences" blend together into a kind of soft white noise through which, now and then, you pick up a cosmic inkling—the real Rilke at work. In "Funeral," he writes:

> Among the fast machines
> which, rapacious and annoyed,
> cross the new-made void
> of unconquerable space,
> passes the slow slug of a funeral . . .
> But the stars are slower still

Poet as Narcissus

Biographer Donald Prater pulls off quite a trick in *A Ringing Glass,* doing a good job of persuading us that Rainer Maria Rilke was "perhaps the greatest lyric genius of our century," while simultaneously providing conclusive testimony that, personally-speaking, his subject was every bit as precious and self-absorbed as he appears in the photo on the cover of this book. Prater's Rilke is proof once again that in aesthetics as in baseball, to paraphrase Leo Durocher's law, you can come in first without being a particularly admirable person.

Born in Prague in 1875, a child of the exhausted middle classes, Rilke wrote in German and French, wandered through Europe, and died in Switzerland in 1926. Along the way he won a considerable literary reputation, largely by inveigling his way into the international cultural aristocracy (if only as its plaything). As Prater shows, most of his writing life was spent treading a circuit of patronage that stretched across the literary drawing-room society of the continent: Munich, Locarno, Geneva, Venice, Zurich, Bern, Berlin.

Sixty years after his death, Rilke's poems are still working that circuit of high culture and expensive taste, relocated to the New World. Here on the north side of Berkeley, the new Stephen Mitchell translations of his writings sell almost as well as workout videos and gourmet cookbooks. In a society preoccupied with self-fulfillment, he is the perfect poet.

"Know then," wrote Rilke to his lover, Lou Andreas-Salomé, "that art is the road to fulfillment for the individual." The

Review of *A Ringing Glass: The Life of Rainer Maria Rilke* by Donald Prater, *Los Angeles Herald Examiner,* 1986.

"vaulting arch" of art, he told her, soars "high above the people." To him, art was not for everybody, only for the sensitive few—himself and those fellow "solitaries" who provided the necessary opposing poles where his "arch" could touch down. The artist, Rilke believed, dwells alone in pristine creative solitude, pondering his soul and at the same time saving it.

His long search for the "ideal woman," biographer Prater shows, was doomed from the start, at least in real-life terms. "An incomparable spinner of words, he could find expression for love in a thousand images and transcendent flights of emotion that made him irresistible [to women], but to give what its reality demanded remained impossible for him." "Love lives on words," the Russian poet Marina Tsvetayeva pointedly advised him in a letter, "and dies with deeds." "This remark," comments Prater, "could well epitomize Rilke's inability to reconcile love with work." Judging by the evidence he turns up in Rilke's life, there was never any contest, love having been left behind at the gate except as subject matter for the poet's transcendent verses.

Prater argues convincingly that each of the principal themes in Rilke's work—the ideal of love without possession, of the Prodigal Son beseeching others not to love him, of the happiness of those who die young, and of marriage as a mutual preservation of solitude—are objectifications of the poet's personal self-involvement. "These ideas," says Prater, were "developed early, and held forth as doctrines to the end of [Rilke's] life; they all reflect the fundamental narcissism of his work. Striving toward inwardness, his poetry remains essentially personal and self-centered, however paradigmatically presented. His letters, beneath the charm, the touches of humor, the empathy with his correspondent, and the philosophical flights, reveal the same eternal preoccupation with himself, his art, and his recurring existential crises."

The "selectivity" of Rilke's literary executors, Prater says, was long responsible for perpetuating "the image of the poet as high priest and philosopher which the work *in vacuo* tended to foster: a being whose earthly life is largely irrelevant, and about whom everything . . . is 'conducive to hyperbole and to the evolution of legends.' "

In his effort to deflate the hyperbole and undo the legends, Prater has enjoyed an advantage not available to earlier biographers in English: the recent discovery and/or publication of important memoirs and correspondence. Access to these allows Prater to deliver a much larger comprehension of the person behind the poems than we've previously had. That person turns out to be neither high priest nor philosopher, but a struggling artist/aesthete with constant money troubles, a perpetual guest, finicky, sickly, neurasthenic, complaining bitterly in letters if hosts abbreviate his writing time by requiring his presence at table after dinner, or if a sawmill is built in the neighborhood, its racket cutting into his concentration like a "great stupid Gillette blade."

The sawmill comment is a telling one. Rilke instinctively associated commerce with distraction, an annoying tug away from the mirror of his poetry. It was a mirror he spent most of his life staring into, seeking his soul's deepest reflections.

A Public Man

It's a sizeable event in the history of poetry when a poet acknowledged in schools and anthologies as "major" decides he wants to take back those famous verses and write them differently.

John Crowe Ransom went to the lengths of lifting his unexpurgated early verses from the library shelves of his home campus, Kenyon College. W. B. Yeats and W. H. Auden, while less thoroughgoing in carrying out the terms of their own poetic purges, were no easier on their early poems. There is good reason for suggesting that these poets were merely acting out the effects of mid-life crises, and should have had their hands tied behind their backs, leaving their poems safe for posterity.

Stephen Spender has come around, in his seventies, to attacking his own work with at least as much severity as the poets mentioned above. Unlike the others, however, he does so not only with excellent justification but with salutary results.

To understand what Spender has done with his poems, one first has to see why he has done it. Even a quick glance into the anthologies—or into his 1955 *Collected*—supplies the answers. It's hard not to be struck by the tendency of Spender's poems to subvert their own compassionate, socially-conscious arguments with romantic imagery of brute physical strength and "energy." This energy is often symbolized by large machines or industrial installations: all those sleek, plunging, piston-

---

Review of *Collected Poems 1928–1985* by Stephen Spender and *Journals 1939–1983* by Stephen Spender, edited by John Goldsmith, *San Francisco Chronicle,* 1986.

pumping express trains, "beautiful" and "huge" gliding airliners and pylons "bare like nude, giant girls that have no secret." (The sensible query of a feminist in the audience at one of the poet's American readings—"Why not like nude giant *men?*"—made enough of an impression on him to find its way into the *Journals.*)

One might even argue that in theory the tension between Spender's struggle to give these poems a fixed, classical surface, and the burden of meaning pressing through from beneath, is the most interesting thing about them. But in practice this gesturing toward a Germanic-heroic sort of Power reduces to an impression of theatricality.

The most famous of the early poems now seem as histrionic as they are technically proficient. Their self-consciousness is like that of an actor rehearsing before a mirror; they roll off the tongue in one lapidary "great line" after another, as if in competition with the immortals. ("I think continually of those who were truly great.") The blame for this is traceable partly to Spender's over-susceptibility to dominant influences—especially the more misty-eyed aspects of Rilke, and the rhetorical abstractions of Yeats and Auden—and partly to simple youthful confusion. The result is an overreaching style that often causes the poems to break apart under the strain of trying to express what is at best self-contradictory, at worst inexpressible.

One gets the feeling that Spender has come to realize all this, and that the new *Collected* represents his attempt to do something about it before time runs out on him. His revisions are neither cosmetic nor gratuitous. He has simply re-grasped these old poems, seen what they were trying to do in the first place, and made them do a better job of it. ("My aim has always been clarity," he says in his introduction.)

The positive effects of his revisionist strategy can be seen in a characteristic anthology piece from the 1930s, "Perhaps." Here Spender's labors on a local, line-by-line level yield a cumulative outcome that raises the poem from a complex but seriously flawed piece of historical inquiry to a statement of another dimension altogether.

The earlier version's sunken submarine, "a burst bubble filled with water," becomes, in a much sharper figure, a bubble "pricked" by water; its "top-hats orating" by the lake in Geneva are now "plotting" instead, a substitution that replaces a rather silly image with an interestingly sinister one. And the Austrian Socialists' ill-fated revolution, formerly sketched out in the crude symbol "the whale of the future," now becomes "Leviathan / Nosing through icebergs of the Arctic wastes"—an image far broader in implication, significantly enlarging the poem's connotative scope.

Vestiges of Spender's period style, meanwhile—the lugubrious fascination with machinery ("flanges stamping, cutting and unrolling"), the dreamy idealization of male Nordic adolescents ("splendid blonde youths")—have vanished from the poem, thankfully. Now it gets an ending worthy of its prophetic conception, as Spender redeems the conditionality implied by the title with a return to the Lake Geneva of the calculating politicians—"Perhaps some Unknown God is newly risen / Beyond the lake, or crucified / Perhaps our time is / Monstrous with stillness like that Alpine range."

The "our time" of Spender's new version expands the poem beyond its limited and dated thirties ish frame into an ahistorical realm of apocalyptic possibility, equal in sweep to, say, Yeats's "Second Coming"—which is pretty impressive terrain indeed.

For all the interest one may find in Spender's thoughtful reconstruction of his *Collected*, it's also true that in terms of sheer readability the poems are at best an entree to the main course here—the banquet of gossip that is his *Journals*.

"I value the parade, the show, the charm of *appearances*," Spender pauses to note somewhere in mid-feast. "I like to think of life as at least in part a non-stop festivity." These lines strike a chord that runs through the *Journals*; they also say quite a bit about why it makes such fascinating reading. It's hard to think of another literary man's diary so devoted to social surfaces, the savoring and faithful rendering of them.

The Spender we encounter here lives "in a panic about engagements," and seems no less upset when he misses a social date ("I forgot to go to Ambassador Thompson's party on Friday last") than when Robert Lowell gives him a frank, negative assessment of some new poems. He distrusts workaholics, expects his friends to be sociable and suggests that anybody who'd rather work than socialize is an "incomplete person." He chides himself for letting his writing go but, at the drop of an invitation, he's off on a jet: All things can tempt him from his craft.

The verb that best catches the tempo of the *Journals* is "whiz," as in "Then I was whizzed off to the radio station and did a broadcast." (This is in Madras, India, but it might be anywhere.) "Then I was whizzed off in rapid succession to two other places and delivered lectures to audiences utterly stupefied by the combination of heat and me. As I was also."

The self-deprecating humor of that passage is typical of Spender's tone, and it's what sustains him throughout these pages, as he whizzes around the globe in the role of international poetry celebrity and ambassador of creative goodwill. We find him now in Germany, now in Tokyo; briefly then at home in England, where he has an audience with the queen mother, but soon off again to Moscow, where he spends his days talking old times with the super-spy Guy Burgess, or perhaps to New York, where he reads his poems on the Dick Cavett show.

In an early journal note, Spender observes, with some sarcasm, that "whoever cannot change the hidden gold of his most intimate life into the currency of gossip insults society." This is Spender the youthful romantic, whose passionate social conscience still obscures his comprehension of his own social appetites. Later comes the self-knowledge and candor of Spender the "Public Man" (as he calls himself in one of his poem titles), quite averse to insulting society in any way: The "gold" of his inner life is indeed forever washing up on an endless stream of bright talk and social patter.

The journals pan that stream, and they're full of flashy, attention-catching nuggets. *Bon mots* tumble from every page. Characters include, of course, Spender's old cronies Auden and Isherwood (Spender's Auden is a super-punctual oddball obsessed with clocks, his Isherwood a California runaway obsessed with beaches and beachboys); his cofounder at *Horizon*, Cyril Connolly (eulogized here for his brilliance not only in the editorial boardroom but in the bedroom—"lobsters he loved, and next to lobsters, sex"); Igor Stravinsky and T. S. Eliot (Spender records a hilarious hypochondria contest between the two, in which Stravinsky claims his blood is unconscionably thick, while Eliot parries that he has the thinnest blood in the world); and Jackie Onassis (who confides over cocktails that her greatest achievement in life is her recovery of sanity after her "difficult time"—though Spender's not certain whether this confidence is sincere or merely part of an enjoyable "game of good manners").

The most painful moments in these pages are those when the enforced isolation of life at the top turns Spender's diary into a repository of unhappy reflections. Such moments occur mostly in the middle of long, slow poetry-reading tours through the academic backwaters of the New World. Spender earns his living this way, so it's hard to feel too sorry for him; in fact, some of these entries are unintentionally quite funny.

Alone in the Nashville Holiday Inn ("what an inappropriate name!"), for instance, Spender experiences several dark nights of the soul when the phone stubbornly refuses to ring: "No one has communicated with me for at least two days . . . Still here after ten days without anyone in Nashville having invited me even for a drink." The weather's bad, and at night "voices in the next room come magnified" through the ceiling grate. He listens "compulsively" to music on the FM radio, waiting for his paycheck. A dinner invitation from a local millionaire doesn't help; Spender's host is a "huge flatfish" who, over the gold table service, bluntly disparages poets and poetry. The offended guest retreats in a huff—back to the "morgue" that's his temporary home.

Although one can't help sensing the poet has left traces of his soul in a thousand Gideon-Bible-belted motel rooms ("Existence is reduced to a common denominator . . . Mystery is stripped from everything"), and suffered spiritual self-tortures while "gesticulating" behind a hundred glass-screened lecture rostrums ("Mrs. O. suddenly stood up, tinkled a little bell and introduced me, 'the great poet,' etc. I did my spiel . . ."), the final impression of all these short hops and "non-places" is washed away by a single evening back in the cleansing social electricity of New York City.

There, one night, Spender jots down in his journal a description of the painter Robert Motherwell in terms that, by changing the word "art" to "poetry," would apply equally to himself: Motherwell, he writes, is one who "has the air of being a highly successful prince of art with a wide culture, great courtesy." The *Journals* are the engaging autobiography of such a man.

Poetry as a Performing Art

Dylan Thomas died in New York in 1953, at age thirty-nine and in the midst of an American reading tour. His premature death, brought on by booze and a shot of morphine, added fuel to a legend that did not go as gently into that good night as the exhausted poet himself did.

Alcoholic, self-destructive, incapable of facing either life's problems or the self he constructed to deal with them, Thomas gradually effaced his poetry with the blowzy image of Poet with a capital P. It was a spectacle that inspired an entire subsequent generation of poet-exhibitionists to whom—after the example of Dylan—the romance of self-destruction became something both lived through and managed, as one standing outside oneself, flaunting a disturbed personal life for public consumption.

This image Thomas left behind remains far more powerful and influential than his work, whose intrinsic quality never matched his skills as a performer. It is a troubling image, made even more so by the thousand-plus pages of begging, whining, cajoling, lying, fawning, manipulating, and self-dramatizing to be found in the *Collected Letters*.

Four times the size of the 1966 *Selected Letters,* this volume is notable first of all for its sheer bulk. Dylan Thomas wrote too many letters. When he heard about Alec Waugh's remark, "Advise Dylan to write more stories and fewer letters," Thomas was irate but undaunted. He often wrote letters in many drafts, and usually for very specific reasons, as in those cases where he

Review of *The Collected Letters of Dylan Thomas,* edited by Paul Ferris, *San Francisco Chronicle*, 1986.

addressed financial patrons or enlisted supporters to organize campaigns aimed at getting him grants. And the present editor, Thomas-biographer Paul Ferris, has left out very little. Many (but not all) of Thomas's most interesting communications have been available for years. With Ferris's scraping of the barrel, as he candidly admits in his introduction, "the proportion of commonplace letters increases."

Ferris's principal contribution to the Thomas legend—and to our understanding of the man—is in his assembling, from disparate sources, a major group of Thomas letters to his wife Caitlin. There are thirty-eight of these, thirty-two of which were previously unpublished. In his writings to Caitlin the glaring weaknesses of Thomas's character come through in all their primary thematic colors, yielding a portrait not of "the artist as fallen angel" (Ferris's term for Dylan) but of the poet as sad, insecure faker.

The dialectic of Thomas's poems—proceeding by images from conflict to conflict, as he explains in one of these letters—is a clear reflection of the dialectic of the writer's character, a complex playing-out of oppositions: shrewdness, innocence, egotism, vulnerability, brilliance, dishonesty, sensitivity, with an instinctive movement toward "liberty" (or self-indulgence) providing the motor that drives the whole thing along.

Thomas described this drive with exuberance in his early correspondence, especially when at age eighteen he wrote to fellow aspiring-poet Pamela Hansford Johnson. "The artist . . . is a law unto himself," he proclaimed. Just after his nineteenth birthday, in 1933, he explained to her his notion of "Functional Anarchy": "*Everything* is wrong that forbids the freedom of the individual." He returned to this theme a few years later in letters to Caitlin Macnamara, a young Irish girl whom he'd met in London. "You're the only person," he wrote her, "with whom I'm entirely free." At that time Thomas was a recent escapee from the "smug darkness" of his Welsh provincial home, adrift in bohemian circles of a London he saw as a "city of the restless dead." Against that kind of backdrop, Caitlin seemed to him an angelic messenger, and he married her.

It was a stormy union from the first. "We'll always be young and unwise together," he told her proudly. But as his precocious career propelled him from the overnight sensation of *18 Poems,* published when he was just twenty, to a spreading chaos in his personal and financial affairs that eventually overcame him, the "unwisdom" Thomas had promulgated came back to haunt him time after time.

With no fixed income, a wife and three hungry children, and "To hell with everything except the inner necessity for expression" as his motto, Thomas hardly qualified as the ideal provider. He soon fell into the humiliating habit of writing begging letters, an art at which he was a virtuoso. "You don't know, do you, any rich person I can try now?" he asked a friend in 1938. "I'll dedicate my next poems to him, & write a special sponger's song." A year later he'd grown even blunter, boasting to a friend that he'd "sooner smarm like a fart licking spaniel than starve in a world of fat bones."

Hand in hand with what Thomas jokingly called his "cadgery" went a major talent for backstabbing. Particularly subject to his attacks were the same editors and publishers he was dunning constantly for "advances." Since they rarely delivered, these parties soon became, in Thomas's letters, everything from "ostentatious vulgar little runt" (Geoffrey Grigson) to "cliché-riddled humbug and pie-fingering hack" (Richard Church, his editor at the company that published his poetry).

Nor were his fellow writers exempt from the forked-tongue technique of Dylan's epistles. Edith Sitwell, in an early letter, was "a poisonous thing of a woman" who wrote "virgin dung." Later she received effusive letters of gratitude, Thomas's way of acknowledging her service in advancing his interests—by funding his 1947 trip to Italy, among other things.

Those badmouthed in the mails by the "marvelous boy" (as Wordsworth called an earlier seven days' wonder of poetry, Thomas Chatterton) became legion. Stephen Spender was another notable target. "The Rupert Brooke of Depression," Thomas called Spender, who responded characteristically by coming to Dylan's rescue in several bad financial scrapes. Spender also helped Thomas avoid conscription during the war by finding him work in propaganda-film studios. The

Spender case was not atypical; Thomas never hesitated to seek the sympathy and assistance of someone he'd disparaged in letters for years, if the moment demanded it.

But private donations and fees for radio and film work never kept Thomas more than a step ahead of creditors, and not always that far. His penchant for drinking up his earnings became a principal feature in the legend. "I spent all the Persian money on beetroot vodka, glycerine beer [and] unveiled ugly women," he wrote to a friend from Teheran, where in 1951 he was working on a film script commissioned by Anglo-Iranian Oil. Before and after, of course, came the well-documented scenes of a similar nature in the New World—New York and points west, where the legend grew along with the damage.

By 1952, his marriage was a wreck, but he depended on Caitlin to the end. When she found a begging letter he'd written to another woman, combining themes of "cadgery" and adultery, he wrote her a squirming, abject missive of apology: "I wanted to see what foul dripping stuff I could hurt myself to write in order to fawn for money . . ."

Finally there were the trembling times when simply getting out of bed in the morning was too much for Thomas's toxin-packed system. On such days, "The ordinary moment . . . of opening doors or letters, speaking good-days to friends or strangers, looking out of windows, making telephone calls" became "so inexplicably (to me) dangerous . . ." Such times ran together, submerged finally in "that old fear of death" as it slowly reeled him in.

This is a sad book. The pathos of the poet's decline, as displayed in these letters, is so strong that self-parody never seems far away; nor does the element of calculation. The Dylan Thomas we find here is reminiscent of nothing so much as the Dylan-simulacrum, "Ern Malley," a hoax-poet concocted by some professors in Australia at the apogee of Thomas's fame. The instant acceptance won by the rhetorically intense, surreal, symbol-laden pseudo-poems of "Malley" said a lot about Thomas's own success. Over time it became hard to tell which was the greater hoax, the comic send-up created by those professors Down Under, or the "real" poet himself.

Protecting a Legend

These are strange times. Even the woods-wise, homefire-burning, American-as-apple-pie poet laureate of the New Frontier, Robert Frost, has been turned into a "monster"—by his own authorized Pulitzer Prize–winning "official" biographer, yet. And all out of personal malice.

This, anyway, is the charge leveled by veteran East Coast writer and editor Stanley Burnshaw, a longtime, long-distance Frost admirer who worked with him as a Holt editor in the poet's final years. Burnshaw later looked on with horror as his own company issued the three volumes of authorized biographer Lawrance Thompson's "literary defamation" of Frost.

Thompson's "fabrication of the 'monster' myth," as Burnshaw calls it, is the subject of this "now-it-can-be-told" tale of the strange tides of biographical revisionism. Burnshaw gets to it by taking the slow way around, supplying first an extended biographical memoir of Frost. This is largely second-hand stuff, necessarily, since the memoir per se covers only the five years or so in which Frost and Burnshaw were in actual contact, or approximately 1/18th of the poet's life. The rest of the story is filled in with broad brushstrokes, using materials gathered from the literary grapevine and from the storehouse of published Frostiana, including, inevitably, the writings of Thompson, the "monster"-fabricator himself.

Thompson's books, in fact, hover over the pages of *Robert Frost Himself* like a huge question mark. The question they pose is resolved only partly here. How could the man that

---

Review of *Robert Frost Himself* by Stanley Burnshaw, *San Francisco Chronicle*, 1986.

Frost himself chose in 1939 to follow him and write his life have turned out to be so totally wrong about him? After all, Thompson observed Frost at extremely close quarters for more than two decades. How do we equate this "monster" that is Thompson's Frost—the self-promoting, lying, devious, manipulative "madman" who says "we always get forward as much by hating as by loving" and then proceeds to do so, climbing the backs of those close to him and leaving a trail of spent lives in his wake—with Burnshaw's Frost, who is unfailingly wise and generous, full of witty, "easeful" conversation yet possessed of a natural sense of authority, always doing or saying the Right Thing, and "accepting himself" for it?

Burnshaw does his best to keep from glancing over his shoulder at the leering skeletons Thompson sprang out of the Frost closet, beating them back whenever they threaten to encroach on the Frost of the greeting cards and anthologies. Frost's public self, the one he helped promote, is the one Burnshaw knows most about. When Thompson suggests to him in private that the poet's apparent nervousness on camera at Kennedy's Inauguration is actually an attempt to "steal the show from the president," Burnshaw is horrified. He never gets over the shock, dating his recognition of "the real Thompson" from this moment.

It's Frost in Camelot who stars here. National sweetheart as well as national poet, he's "feted wherever he goes"—even Israel, which he regards "as a sort of American colony." In Jerusalem, as everywhere, his "hosts would stand on their heads to please him." Burnshaw helps, flying ahead to Israel to tip off the hosts about Frost's little likes ("ginger ale, with rum if possible") and dislikes ("I advised against praising other poets").

Burnshaw is never quite sure what Frost really feels about all these State Department banquets in his honor, the testimonial tributes, the cabinet-level, after-dinner speakers. When, at one party thrown for the poet by Stewart Udall, the speakers—Earl Warren, Felix Frankfurter, Adlai Stevenson—run on, Burnshaw glances at Frost and wonders, "What can it mean to him now?"

What Frost did feel at such moments remains a mystery. Thompson gave us a negative Frost, Burnshaw a positive one, but what about the hidden, "secret" Frost? You get the feeling that the "secret" Frost took those public occasions for exactly what they were, publicity, something one did to sell books and make a living. Robert Frost clearly refused to elevate himself above the common American in at least one important respect: He never considered himself exempt from what he called in a poem "The trial by market everything must come to."

Whoever the real Frost is or was, Stanley Burnshaw charges that the petty, egotistical old coot left in people's minds by Lawrance Thompson bears no resemblance to him. Thompson, he says, was guilty of massive bias against Frost, whom he'd gradually come to loathe.

This contention is well supported and substantiated here, complete with documents on file at the office of the publisher, as Burnshaw informs us. He brings evidence of various kinds against Thompson: There's corroboration from a critic Thompson once approached with dirt on Frost ("the REAL truth about that monster"). There's corroboration from Thompson's research notes, which Burnshaw has dug up and produces as proof of Thompson's lack of "dependability" and "unreasonable distrust and suspicion" of Frost. There's in-house documentation from the files of Holt, where Burnshaw worked when the firm was publishing first Frost and then Thompson.

And, most tellingly, there's private testimony from Frost himself. In 1959, the poet told Burnshaw unexpectedly: "I'm counting on you to protect me from Larry" (i.e., from Thompson) and later made it plain to him that he'd grown afraid of Thompson, had deliberately misled the biographer in order to "befuddle" and "confuse" him and now feared this treatment had only increased the "hate" and "resentment" of his adversary. If at this point "Frost were to break the relationship" (i.e., "fire" Thompson), Burnshaw points out, he would "surrender all constraints over Thompson." Thompson could then say anything he wanted in an "unauthorized" biography.

The poet had a choice between "two risks"—fire Thompson and risk his ire posthumously or keep him on and try to outlive it and/or him.

Feeling Thompson's biographical grasp closing around his throat, Frost didn't so much choose the latter course as delay and procrastinate himself into it. It became a contest of who could live longer, he or his biographer, and Frost lost this one. But then, in the great dialectic of publishing history, there remained Burnshaw—who'd been in the thick of things at Holt, and obviously knew everything—to contend with. Thompson lost that one. He died in 1977, and Burnshaw wrote this book.

The Romance of Damage

When twenty-one-year-old John Wieners arrived at Black Mountain College in 1955, both Charles Olson and Robert Duncan were, as Duncan recalls, awed by the "sheer authenticity" of the young newcomer's talent. But this true original of American poetry remained less well-known than many of the Beat and Black Mountain poets who were his associates, largely because of his own shy and retiring personality.

Now, *The Selected Poems: 1958–1984* collects all Wieners's major work (most of it very hard to find in the original editions).

Here in their entirety are *The Hotel Wentley Poems* (1958), a San Francisco sequence that became a modern classic ("a tragic *maudit*," Allen Ginsberg called the Wieners of *Hotel Wentley*); *Ace of Pentacles* (1964), with its uptown New York diamond store dreams and flash of imagination illuminating smoke-ringed rooms where "one goes / up the angelic ladder" to "rise again in the dawn"; *Pressed Wafer* (1967), which stated Wieners's poetic calling—"There are holy orders in life. / I was born to be a priest / defrocked . . . to make manifest mysteries"; *Asylum Poems* (1969), with its echoes of personal chaos: "When the shadows enlarge . . . What will one do, how"; and *Nerves* (1970), a volume whose courage, grace and cool intelligence cut like sapphire "down the line" into "a sexual kind / of nightmare." Also included are selections from *Behind the State*

Review of *The Selected Poems: 1958–1984* by John Wieners, foreword by Allen Ginsberg, edited by Raymond Foye, and *The Book of Nods* by Jim Carroll, *San Francisco Chronicle*, 1986.

Capitol (1975), many unpublished or uncollected poems, and two interviews with the poet.

In one of the interviews, Wieners (whose Catholic upbringing didn't save him from drug dependency, the traumatic breakup of a longstanding homosexual love affair, serious attacks of depression and electric-shock treatments) tells the interviewer, "Poems . . . are my salvation alone." The theme of redemption through art and suffering has rarely been expressed as eloquently as in Wieners's "The Acts of Youth":

> And with great fear I inhabit the middle of the night
> What wrecks of the mind await me, what drugs
> to dull the senses, what little I have left,
> what more can be taken away?
>
> Pain and suffering. Give me the strength
> to bear it, to enter those places where the
> great animals are caged. And we can live
> at peace by their side. A bride to the burden
>
> that no god imposes but knows we have the means
> to sustain its force unto the end of our days.
> For that is what we are made for; for that
> we are created. Until the dark hours are done.
>
> And we rise again in the dawn.
> Infinite particles of the divine sun, now
> worshipped in the pitches of the night.

The intricate lyricism and elegance of surface in Wieners's best poems triumph over illness, pain and loneliness. And sometimes he achieves a lotus-eater's perfection of vision, in poems as fragile and serene as a Chinese vase painting: "Birds of paradise float in green lagoons, / while painted canopies stretch over Chinese couples / sunning themselves in gowns of feathered silk . . . / Boats are propelled by poles of bamboo, / held in the hands of dreamers; the holds are heavy / with fruit and dates; and they paddle through clouds / of azure drifting in canals of heaven" ("Chinoiserie").

If John Wieners's work prefigured the romance of damage for our time, Jim Carroll's embodies it. Dantesque, glittering, sensuous and destructive, the neon-lit dark sea floor of modern urban life takes on similar characteristics of alienation, narcosis and exaltation in both these poets' writings. They are, respectively, the Baudelaire and Rimbaud of twentieth-century American poetry.

Rimbaud, indeed, has been Jim Carroll's personal poetic ideal and private doppelgänger ever since his adolescent years in the 1960s, when, despite the distractions of being a teenage basketball hero and heavy-duty heroin addict, he began writing poetry. He survived that risky youth to become a grown-up rock and roll star, with several successful albums to his credit. And more important, a writer, whose amazing prose memoir, *The Basketball Diaries,* became a bestseller, and whose second collection of poems, *The Book of Nods,* establishes him, at thirty-five, as a mature and poised poet.

The fact that through all this he's never abandoned his original precariousness of approach—his way of fusing life and art into a tightwire across the abyss—is what makes Jim Carroll's identification with Rimbaud seem less like a mere literary fancy than an affinity of the soul.

Like Rimbaud's, the angels in Carroll's poems have reality-singed wings; they are "radiant swallows, or hummingbirds," whose illuminations take place, if not in an Inferno, then in some "blank and dumb" Purgatory—"that Limbo [where] the children move / in some strange gravity within and / outside grace. Their Lord is angry . . . Do you understand / what I am saying? It is the life you chose / on this earth. The life of junk and lies" ("For Elizabeth").

Hanging in the limbo of the present, Jim Carroll doesn't so much mourn the loss or denial of grace as transfigure it through recognition. His poems' urgent, obsessive metaphors are posed tensely against their cool, streetwise surface voice, charging them with an electricity that's at once sexual, religious and disturbingly psychological.

Take the poem "Saint Theresa" ("Her tiny heart / pierced on a thorn / heats the jealous rose above it"). Or the strange de Sade–like demonstration of inverse theology with which Carroll concludes the prose poem sequence "Rimbaud Scenes"—

"Rimbaud spoke: 'Now the history of Christ's death rests in my body, and will pass through me by morning! Tell me, what poison could be more exquisite?'" ("Rimbaud Pays Homage to Saint Helena"). This is the poet who called one of his rock albums *Catholic Boy!*

Subway Troubadour

Some of the best of our poetry comes out of the late 1950s and early 1960s, a time when the discoveries of William Carlos Williams and Ezra Pound were approaching full realization in the work of a group of younger writers intent on keeping the language equally true, fresh and alive. One of the talented young progressives of that period was New York poet Paul Blackburn, whose early allegiance to Williams and Pound (both of whom he'd befriended by mail while still a college student) had brought him into contact with writers of his own generation like Charles Olson and Robert Creeley. Along with Olson, Creeley and other writers of the Black Mountain group, Blackburn devoted himself to exploring and extending the Pound/Williams breakthrough—in so doing, creating a whole new terrain for American poetry.

That's one area of the culture where the maps keep changing constantly, however. By the 1970s, Blackburn's innovative work was already hard to find, scattered through ephemeral, often out-of-print volumes that hadn't been easy to turn up even when new. Reading Blackburn became impossible for anyone lacking the hours (or the dollars) of a serious collector. All that changes now, with the 523 poems lovingly and laboriously assembled by Edith Jarolim into this copious *Collected*—a book that gives us the first organized body of work by which to assess this prolific writer.

Blackburn died in 1971, at age forty-four, of a cancer that came almost as an objectification of the longing for uncon-

Review of *The Collected Poems of Paul Blackburn,* edited, with an introduction, by Edith Jarolim, *Los Angeles Times*, 1986.

sciousness, the deathward swoon, expressed in much of his later poetry. "Suffering is what happens / when you can't feel what is there," he'd written in the poem "Repetitions." "Suffering is induced, imposed, asked for. Liquor, drugs / are understandable attempts to not feel / pain." For this poet committed to the ideal of Eros, Death was the ultimate lover, a final tunnel of extinction "at spur's end" beyond the "nets of lust" and the last BMT stop—releasing one into "the jaw of what softness we rut toward . . . To roll into it / and stay there warm" ("Baggs").

The vision in many of Blackburn's poems may be as dark as a subway tunnel, but the voice is always clear. His early immersion in the regular-guy, man-on-the-street discourse of William Carlos Williams (experienced tough guy wearing heart on T-shirt sleeve, tucked in next to pack of Camels) had a permanently salutary effect, keeping Blackburn's poems as honestly expressive and democratically engaging as the pluralistic urban society whose surfaces they reflect. Confidential, wry, knowing, but somehow modest—the Blackburn voice is always there, as easy to trust as a loyal friend.

Blackburn kept the man-on-the-street modesty as his standard. "To write poems, say, / is not a personal achievement," he suggests in one poem, thereby dismissing his own years of careful practice with a single calculated shrug, as if to say, "anyone can do it." (But of course, anyone can't, as Blackburn well knew.) Or again: "Poems will not do. / It is a kind of minuteness of application of whatever blessed / things the goddess has put in our hands" ("Winter Solstice").

Blackburn found that his own dalliance with "the goddess," both in her divine and too-human manifestations, brought its special costs. "Wounded so many times by love" in his poems, in real life he went through three wives and numerous temporary attachments, repeatedly bouncing back up, only to be pulled down into the whirlpool-vertigo of love (or "lust," as he called it in an unconscious echo of his Catholic upbringing) all over again.

It was as if not only in poetry but in reality Blackburn had to live out the Provencal troubadour poet-lover's fate of heart-loss and perpetual victimization at the feet of the remote, cruel, Unkind Lady. Adopting this troubadour persona as a distancing device for a mock-plaintive lyricism, he used poetry to give him courage in love, and vice versa—remaining willing to "risk / that evil thing / wherein our own heart go forth from us," even though wise enough to acknowledge that "Love is a weakness, a / sickness, a fear & a terror" ("O Do That Medieval Thing Again, Baby").

In his last years, Blackburn abandoned the strict form of his poems in favor of a looser-structured kind of verse "journal," which gradually became a diaristic catch-all for his daily doings, domestic life, travels and creative process. This increasingly painful poetic home movie keeps rolling almost to the bitter end, as we see the dying poet surveying his wasted body in the bath, "waiting for the ache . . . to go away."

"Let / each man's words be his own," he writes a few months before death, echoing the close of one of his finest early poems, "The Dissolving Fabric," about a suicide: "she possessed her own life, and took it." The self-possession always to be found at the center of Blackburn's poetry, holding it all together with a steady, controlled presence, was the last thing to leave him. In the poems, it remains.

Urban Illuminations

When the New York poet and critic Edwin Denby died three years ago at the age of eighty, few people west of the Hudson River were aware that America had lost one of its finest writers. Denby was one of those rare beings: an artist who not only failed to court public attention for his work but, guided by a natural reticence, actively shunned it.

The "Complete" in this book's title, therefore, might have been as accurately "Recovered" or "Rescued." These poems have appeared earlier, but only in small, obscure editions subsidized by Denby himself or by his numerous friends and admirers.

In his introduction, editor Ron Padgett details Denby's efforts to efface himself as an artist, and to deflect whatever recognition came to him through his poetry. Denby, Padgett says, "never 'built his career' as a poet. He never did anything to make his poetry known to a wide audience. In fact, by the 1960s he had become skittish about having his poetry published at all . . ."

Denby began to write verse in his teens and went on doing so into the early 1960s, after which time he produced very little. His formal approach remains remarkably uniform throughout his work, from early to late, though in the later poetry the tonal means are much more relaxed, adept and various.

His dominant form is the Shakespearean sonnet, which he employed with spare, reductive intensity and a skillful manipulation of what Padgett terms "compressed, quirky, big-city stop-

---

Review of *The Complete Poems* by Edwin Denby, edited and with an introduction by Ron Padgett, *San Francisco Chronicle*, 1986.

and-go rhythms." The key is the compression, creating the effect of a dense, spoken prosody, something like an American version of Gerard Manley Hopkins's sprung rhythm. But Denby's range of feeling is broader than Hopkins's. In a Denby poem voices and inflections can shade into one another as subtly and quickly as an expressive person's gestures. The poems are nimble, mutable and very often intriguingly elliptical.

The disjunctions and ellipses that give Denby's poetry its tension reflect the "dislocations," as Padgett calls them, of his early life. The son of a consular official, Denby was born in China, reared in Vienna, later dropped out of Harvard, returned to Europe, danced with a German touring company for five years and, for a while, was even a patient of Freud's analytical partner, Federn (who also treated Rilke and Wilhelm Reich).

Back in America, Denby moved next door to Willem de Kooning, with whom he began a long friendship. He soon met and befriended other painters and artists. By 1936 he was working at what became his primary profession, dance criticism. His essays were collected in two books that became classics on the subject, *Looking at the Dance* (1949) and *Dancers, Buildings and People on the Streets* (1965).

"He sees and hears more clearly than anyone else I have ever known," the poet Frank O'Hara said, pointing to the quality of clarity that inheres in both Denby's discursive prose and his poems. Denby's enduring subject, the climate, light, streets and people of New York City, was one to which he brought an exceptional attention.

De Kooning, Denby once wrote, "looked hard to catch exactly what was there." Denby himself did that in all his writing. "Daily life is wonderfully full of things to see," he told a group of New York ballet students in a lecture reprinted in one of his books on dance. "There is no point in living here, if you don't see the city you're living in."

But Denby's way of seeing was less detached than a painter's. "I found I did not see with a painter's eye," he wrote in a memoir about his life in the thirties. "For me the after-image (as Elaine de Kooning called it) became one of the ways people behave together, that is, a moral image."

At first sight, not Pollock, Kline scared
Me, in the Cedar, ten years past
Drunk, dark-eyed, watchful, light-hearted
Everybody drunk, his wide chest
Adorable hero, mourn him
No one Franz didn't like, Elaine said
The flowered casket was loathsome
Who are we sorry for, he's dead
Between death and us his painting
Stood, we relied daily on it
To keep our hearts on the main thing
Grandeur in a happy world of shit
Walk up his stoop, 14th near 8th
The view stretches as far as death.

In one poem Denby wrote of Walt Whitman, "The grand republic's poet is / Brooklyn Whitman, commuter Walt / Nobody else believes all of it." A tender way of *believing all of it* is very close to the essence of Denby's own vision. Also central is a quality of light or grace more akin to Dante, another of his favorite poets.

In his later years Denby often carried with him a volume of the *Divine Comedy*—always the "Purgatorio" or the "Paradiso," as Padgett points out, never the "Inferno." "Disorder, mental, strikes me," he begins one of his final sonnets. "I slip from my pocket Dante to / Chance hit a word, a friend's reply . . . " In the "lunge of headlights" glimpsed from a Sixth Avenue bar "as dawn enters the sunk city," the poet turns to Dante for some "answer a one can understand / Actual events are obscure / Though the observers appear clear."

In personal remarks about the poet, editor Padgett speaks of Denby's "inwardness, surprising in so public a man . . . a kind of radiance or spirituality." It's also there in the poems, which always manage to make out the illuminated moments in the dark wood of a complex, sometimes perilous urban life. To Denby, the illuminations always overshadowed the perils. I remember a letter I had from him twenty years ago. "New York is pure paradise," he wrote, "though the angels two or three feet away terrify."

Total Exposure

James Schuyler is the poet who once compared the "calm secret exultation" of Christmas to the taste of Sealtest eggnog, and in another poem predicted with tongue in cheek that when death came for him it would find him with a jar of Yuban instant coffee in one hand, a jar of Coleman's mustard in the other.

Therefore, it's no surprise to find the long (twenty-seven-page), powerful title poem of his new book, *A Few Days*, packed with similar details of dailiness in a commodity society: The "soft September sun" of New York City turns the air "fizzy like / soda water: Perrier / in the odd-shaped bottle from France"; and the poet reveals that, in his ablutions, he makes do with "Breck's Shampoo for Normal Hair, 40¢ off," but treats himself to cologne that costs "sixteen twenty" a bottle.

Schuyler's total-exposure tactic here extends as far as a disarmingly cheerful inventory of the fine points of his drinking problem and nervous breakdowns, down to exact chemical dosages: "seven Sleepeze, two Nembutal . . . three / antidepressant pills, a red pill that controls the side / effects of the antidepressants."

Mike Wallace once accused William Carlos Williams of making poetry out of his shopping lists. The charge applies as well to Schuyler's work as to Williams's. Like Williams, Schuyler has always been "more interested in truth than in imagination," as he says in *A Few Days*. This poem carries the imprint

Review of *A Few Days* by James Schuyler, *San Francisco Chronicle*, 1986.

of a lover of the literal. But its confessional, sketchbook-like form rambles to a purpose, always circulating around a single theme: mortality, and its traditional poetic antidote, once summed up in the phrase "*carpe diem*," or "seize the day."

"Tomorrow is another day," Schuyler writes. "But no better than today if / you only realize it. / Let's love today, the what we have now, this day, not / today or tomorrow or / yesterday, but this passing moment, that will not / come again."

While Schuyler's modesty and humor, lightness of touch, subtlety of ear and fastidious Intimist-painter's eye are all busy colluding to create the impression that his poem is no more than what it seems—a random, friendly grab bag of daily details—the cohesion of its form is at work at a deeper level, slowly sneaking up on you.

In *A Few Days*, Schuyler records events of scattered days over two months in August and September, 1979. He visits his eighty-nine-year-old mother at the family home in western New York State. He then returns to the big city, where, alone in his apartment, he writes, sleeps, listens to the radio and thinks about the past—a process that weaves into the narrative a new set of locales: Maine, Long Island, Vermont—while getting ready to go out to a dinner party ("my favorite form of entertainment").

After about 1200 long, breezy lines of this gossipy catalog of moments (life's "squandered minutes, hours, days"), the form contracts abruptly: The poet gets news of his mother's death and his poem shifts gears, slipping into a quiet elegiac conclusion that redeems and illuminates the whole carefully elaborated miscellany that has come before. Schuyler's closing lines establish the poem's central relation, between this poet-son ("more interested in truth") and "Mother,"

> enearthed beside
> my stepfather:
> once when I was
> home a while ago
> I said I realized
> that in his way he
> loved me. "He did

not," my mother said,
"Burton hated you."
The old truth-teller!

This is Schuyler's fifth major collection, his first since the Pulitzer Prize–winning *The Morning of the Poem* (1980). In addition to its masterly title piece, it contains forty-nine fine shorter poems, for and about friends, birthdays, places, weather, lovers ("his blond hair / diamond-dusted with / raindrop fragments"), and other significant details of "all this beauty in the / mess" of a bachelor writer's life as lived "on / West Twentieth in Chelsea, New York."

The Gift of Breath

This book's six interlinked sequences of poems arise quietly from, and address gently, concerns that only can be called basic and universal. These are: the condition of motherhood, its joys, fears, mysteries and routine labors; the problems of locating freedom and happiness in a landscape of large-scale social inequity dominated by poverty's crippling dread; and the risky, sometimes desperate, commitment of a singular spirit bent on keeping soul-values alive in a vale of woes.

"Proximity of prayer / is like a little well's / way into the beautiful / black. Here, words drill / a path for a sailing soul" ("Mission Hill").

Though in terms of technique Howe's work is as up-to-date as anybody's (the musicality, concentration, figuration and compression here are impressive), the feeling that bursts forth from it is like a miraculous whiff of fresh air from some other time, some age when art had very different purposes. The breath that animates Howe's poetry seems to blow not from a contemporary world of "materials" and "individuals" but from one of radical mystical belief.

But saying all this makes *Robeson Street* sound medieval, a throwback to the days of St. Theresa or Dame Judith of Norwich. It's not. This is a modern woman speaking. Fanny Howe's self-placement in the contemporary scenes of her poems—the churches, housing projects, zoos, meadows, parks of Boston's urban fringe—occurs with full consciousness of what she's doing there, in all senses including the social.

Review of *Robeson Street* by Fanny Howe, *San Francisco Chronicle*, 1986.

Howe makes it clear that not only economic disenfranchisement but sexual repression afflicts the waiting women in her poems: "Pushing children in plaid & silver prams / us mothers were dumpy, hunched in the damp." But her presentation of motherhood as a condition of voluntary sacrifice and service discriminates it from the involuntary self-suppression of imposed duty. Mothering, here, is rescued by spirit, restored to a state of delight. When Howe asks herself what all this work-for-another really means, the answer leaps out as part of her entire life-resolve: "I . . . knew why it was I was pregnant; / more lips to love lilacs with."

The mystery of life is a difficult one, she seems to say, understood only once it is accepted. And faith in the mystery brings its own intimately grasped revelation, a knowledge of love as the human completion of the whole curve of the universe.

Howe writes in "The Nursery": "And when the baby sighed / through the circle of lips, / I kissed it, / and so did he, my circle to his, / we kissed ourselves and each other / as if each cell was a Cupid, / and we were born in it." The play on "cell," with its double sense of physical unit and metaphorical prison ("invisibly prisoned / in vessels & cords") reflects the kind of multiple awareness that plays around all of Howe's lines giving them a rich plural life.

Pursuing truth and justice with unflagging hopefulness, the poet manages to transfigure both the walled-in isolation of a single motherhood and the proximity of others' similar or worse states. "The suffering of others," that of the sad, estranged women behind prams, or of "the poor who are occluded / and stationary," is always present around the edges of these poems. But love keeps coming in—through the "eyes, and a sudden soul" of a twelve-week-old infant, or the grown-up kind of "Love" that "essays, in the form of Eros / to be at liberty in the dark."

If the latter's "armful of kisses" brings with it hopes "shot / Down with the cold of a faraway Moscow," Howe suggests, so be it: even if "no opiate made so many people poor as pure / desire," still desire is a sign of life; and "Nothing on earth compares with breath."

That "breath" is the real gift of these poems, an aura that

Fanny Howe works to refine until it dazzles. "Simple faith," she writes in one poem, is "a way not given / statement. Wonder sinks to golden / silence." The aura of wonder, an evanescent glow felt in life's best moments, when they seem to point beyond themselves, moves through her poems, hangs in and around them—the emanation of a stubbornly resilient spirit.

Dramatic Voices

Donald Hall's eminence as an editor, teacher and critic of verse has had the unfortunate effect of overshadowing his own poems, an effect enhanced in recent years by his reticence about publishing new work. (This latest collection's his first to appear in eight years.) Hall is an extreme example of the perfectionist poet, one who writes his poems over and over again, until sometimes the copious re-draftings add up to as many pages as the manuscript of a novel. In his pursuit of a poetry worthy of eternity, Hall refuses to settle for near misses.

The Happy Man lives up to Hall's own high standard. His eighth collection of poems in thirty-one years, it marks a major advance for him, particularly in its strategic use of dramatic voices.

The longest and most difficult piece here, "Shrubs Burned Away" (one section, Hall informs us in a note, of an even longer work) takes Hall's new dramatic method to its extreme, with a multi-voiced, elliptical narrative that has the disjunct structure of a disturbing dream. The most arresting of its voices is that of a lonely, troubled, middle-aged man who every evening numbs himself with whiskey, in his home or out in the faceless neon American motel night.

This troubled man's voice is a kind of ground bass in *The Happy Man,* making its title deeply ironic. If the man in "Shrubs Burned Away" tells himself, six scotches down the line, that he's "very happy," it's clearly a precarious happiness,

Review of *The Happy Man* by Donald Hall, *San Francisco Chronicle,* 1986.

the thin ice over waters of breakup and breakdown whose chill is almost tangible.

That voice comes back in two impressive dramatic monologues at the center of the book, "My Friend Felix" and "Merle Bascom's .22." The former's middle-aged narrator, driving across Texas, is joined by the apparition of an old friend who's been dead thirty years—"my lucky friend Felix." A sudden brush with automotive death coaxes a revelatory message out of this ghost, just as a crash is averted at the last moment. The brush with highway death recurs in "Merle Bascom's .22," where the association of sudden death with revelation is even closer.

Conflicting senses of mortality are currents that govern this book. Hall alternately proposes the sweet temptation of death as ultimate release, and the dread and grief of death as terminal closure; they are emotional pulls which he wisely allows to remain in tension, unresolved and unreconciled in these poems as they are in life.

The New Hampshire farm poems early in *The Happy Man* show Hall's pastoral understanding; in the later poems the pastoral image is threatened by other images, darker ones that close in by stages, like wolves encircling a pasture at twilight. The poems show a love of the sun, the upward process of growth, and the green fields of daylight—but also a strong sense of a very different kind of natural force, which pulls at us from the other direction.

This downward pull is embodied with reductive eloquence in the dramatic figuration of the book's finest pieces—like the small lament for ex-baseball hero Ted Williams on Old Timers' Day, "Couplet," where Williams, lumbering to catch a fly ball, becomes a fallen god, a divine warrior brought low by time's gravity on the bright playing surface / battlefield: "we rise," Hall writes, "and applaud weeping: / On a green field / we observe the ruin / of even the bravest / body, as Odysseus / wept to glimpse / among the shades the shadow / of Achilles."

The craftsmanship for which Donald Hall's often been praised is responsible for maneuvering the syntax of those lines so adroitly, but the elegiac power there is something new for this fine poet.

Creating Paradise

> Sweetheart, I wish you could tour my native land.
> . . . and love me in context.
>
> ("Travelogue")

The dramatic voices of these poems are metaphors for states of the soul seeking its context. They are given existence by a writer whose most salient gift is her awesome capacity for surrendering authorial identification with the voicing of the work.

Amy Gerstler's dreams of healing and union are projected into "selves"—themselves metaphors of her intent, which is no less than to create a white and blameless paradise wherein our visions, terrors and desires merge together in the purity of our imagining them.

On December 17, 1817, the poet John Keats and several friends went to see a Christmas pantomime at Drury Lane. Walking back to Hampstead, Keats engaged in a "disquisition" with his friend Dilke. In the days preceding this conversation Keats had been thinking much about Shakespeare and the idea of dramatic voices as masks.

"Several things dove-tailed in my mind," he reported soon afterwards in a letter to his brother in America, "& at once it struck me, what quality went to form a Man of Achievement especially in Literature & which Shakespeare possessed so enormously—I mean *Negative Capability,* that is when man is capable of being in uncertainties, Mysteries, doubts, without an irritable reaching after fact & reason . . . This pursued

---

Introduction to *The True Bride* by Amy Gerstler (Lapis Press, 1986).

through volumes would perhaps take us no further than this, that with a great poet the sense of Beauty overcomes every other consideration, or rather obliterates all considerations."

> I should know more about the sky
> after all this time on my back . . .
>
> ("Christine")

"The only means of strengthening one's intellect is to make up one's mind about nothing—to let the mind be a thoroughfare for all thoughts," Keats said in another letter written shortly after the Negative Capability note.

The best test of how much light a poet is directing in his or her poem is whether the beam of his or her attention on his or her chosen subjects also illuminates things around this strangely androgynous space they create, crystallizing and giving shape not only to the subjects themselves but to the whole field of surrounding objects, making those too glow with shared clarity. In opening one cell of reality, the true poet's attention spills over and penetrates the next. This process of overflowing operates all through Amy Gerstler's work.

Traditionalist at the Beach

Reading this highly regarded young Los Angeles poet's second book of poems I was reminded of a comment made by the great Irish bard W. B. Yeats on the occasion of his visit to Southern California in the 1930s. "Here if anywhere else in America," Yeats said, "I seem to hear the coming footsteps of the Muses."

Given the historical output of Los Angeles poets—not exactly an enormous one—one is tempted to wonder whether Yeats, after saying that, went home and smooched the blarney stone for a week. The tantalizing potential of Southern California for poets, though, has long been obvious. When Gene Stratton Porter arrived here from Indiana in 1919, she found herself "forced to utterance" by "something in the wonderful air, the gorgeous color on all hands and the pronouncedly insistent rhythms." But as cultural critic Carey McWilliams later pointed out, local poetic utterances for too long remained "forced." Southern California poets, McWilliams suggested some forty years ago, have had trouble fitting their verses to the place where they live, too often lacking "the wit to recognize the existence of a cultural problem."

The "cultural problem" is that of any desperately heterogeneous culture that can't grasp its roots because it doesn't have any. What kind of verse do you use to capture the poetry of a vast artificial jungle planted in the middle of a desert?

Timothy Steele's finest poems provide one answer to that question, yielding a credible image of the dense, sprawling,

Review of *Sapphics Against Anger and Other Poems* by Timothy Steele, *Los Angeles Herald Examiner,* 1986.

half-tropical, half-megalopolitan culture from which they spring. Steele's best asset as a poet of this place is what might be called a California attitude—pleasure-oriented, laid-back, sense-receptive. In the face of life's "rebuffs," he's always willing to trust that:

> the senses still will solve
> The fuzzy scent and surface of a peach.
> Joys will return, a beachball will revolve
> Breeze-prompted colors down a slope of beach.

His poems record a resolute pursuit of the pleasures of a material world whose abundant surfaces are made real in the language. They celebrate "the abstract beauty of the world," as in "At Will Rogers Beach," a poem that catches the panorama of Southern California life as a whirl of shape and color—surfers, fishermen, lifeguards, dogs chasing Frisbees and roller skaters "Translating into speed their form and weight." Tim Steele has his bad nights, his "terrors of the dark," but this is a poet whose natural bent is to stay hopeful, positive and ever-ready to enjoy life in the sunlight, while it lasts.

In "From a Rooftop" he peers down at the recumbent city "relaxed to sounds and shapes," a Mondrian-geometry of "long streets with traffic signals blinking red." In "Near Olympic" he moves in closer, observing a "neighborhood, part Japanese, part Chicano" that "wears its poverty like art." This poem is a beautiful registration of locale.

> Over dirt driveways hang banana trees;
> In front of small square stucco houses bloom
> Broad jacarandas whose rain-washed perfume
> At morning half redeems the rush-hour released
> Swelled roaring of the freeway six blocks east.

Steele observes the human landscape of West Los Angeles with equal accuracy: Idle young men drinking beer while acid rock blasts from a van; "Carlos, chief dude of the rec center" surveying the scene, his "mind on Mexico."

Steele's supple handling of traditionally measured verse

forms, whose discursive capacities he exploits to stake out carefully designed arguments, show him to be a humanist-classicist at heart. Pompous moments ("The nominalist in me invents / A life devoid of precedents") mar some of the poems, and a too-easy facility undermines others. Suave, smooth, sometimes a little bland, Steele's verse possesses the kind of jauntily sanguine attitude and deft surface polish that guarantee success in neo-formalist academic quarters. One hopes he'll not ignore the Muses of that native ground where his best poems—with their way of touching momentarily "a durable, elusive energy" that's "here and gone . . . pure presence and repose . . . mere lovely being"—come from.

Identified Flying Objects

Poet Bob Kaufman, who wrote like a black hipster angel, completed his term on this planet only two weeks into this year. My guess, from the sad shape he was in the last time I saw him, is that 1986 wouldn't have been much of a year for Bob anyway. The hundreds who paid tribute to this legendary figure in the weeks after his death—at a funeral service, cremation, ash-scattering and tender parade of poets through North Beach—were honoring the memory of a man who died forgotten by American Poetry, his legend pretty much confined to a dwindling coterie of loyal fans and friends, his work largely unread, unknown and ignored by the academic-structuralist establishment that rules over poetry in the 1980s.

Kaufman survived to the age of sixty-one, well beyond the span of many self-consuming poet-visionaries—including Hart Crane, the poet whose work Kaufman's probably has most in common with. Kaufman's poems resemble Crane's in their rhetorical locutions, their leaps between elliptical, daring images, and (to use Crane's own phrases) their "emotional dynamics" and reliance on a "logic of metaphor."

Kaufman's best poems, though, have something extra—a quality of gentleness and compassion, a radiating of hope and light that relieves the brokenness of experience. In these "metaphysical designs of want and care," as Kaufman once called his poems, things often seem to be hovering at the brink of some ecstatic transformation—a transfiguration of the personal realm into eternal dimensions: "All those ships

---

Review of *Closing Time Till Dawn* by Bob Kaufman and Janice Blue, *San Francisco Chronicle*, 1986.

that never sailed / Today I bring them home and let them sail forever."

Kaufman was not a poet of plush studies and libraries but a troubadour and adventurer, like Villon and Rimbaud. Born in New Orleans, grandson of an African slave, son of a German Jew and a black Catholic woman from Martinique, he grew up talking Cajun, went to sea as a cabin boy at the age of thirteen and did saturation reading in the classics while sailing nine times around the world. A dedicated maritime union man, he later became a Communist labor organizer in the South, where he was badly beaten by police in what was to be one of many major negative encounters with the American legal system. Subsequently, he was arrested dozens of times in San Francisco; in 1963 in New York he was "treated" with electroshock after a spell in the Tombs and Rikers Island.

Soon thereafter, although his poems were influencing everyone from Jack Kerouac to Bob Dylan, and his songs (which he performed in New York clubs and coffeehouses) were getting recorded by the New Christy Minstrels and Chubby Checker, Kaufman entered a self-imposed ten-year silence, lasting from the assassination of John Kennedy to the end of the Vietnam War. Like Antonin Artaud in his decade of confinement, Bob Kaufman in his silent years was perhaps taking on himself the suffering soul of his time ("my body is a torn mattress," he wrote, "I have shot myself with my eyes"), as if the single spirit of a poet could experience and redeem it all.

Closing Time Till Dawn is a small book that looks like ephemera. But, with a poet as modest about publication as Kaufman (he published only three books in his lifetime), even the ephemera bears close scrutiny. In this case the slight, hand-sewn chapbook yields more substance than many volumes of "major" poetry.

It was composed in the middle of one winter night, 1973, at the Tower Hotel on upper Grant Avenue, with Kaufman, who'd just emerged from his long "sabbatical of silence," being literally coaxed into poetry by his collaborator, Janice Blue. Blue, says publisher-poet Paul Landry in an attached note, "tricked Bob into writing by telling him they had to be quiet since I was sleeping." The result is an extended conversation poem, the two poets trading verses that read like a lyrical, funny and (thanks to Kaufman) occasionally metaphysical/romantic dialogue between man and woman—with the former, in Landry's terms, "hustling," and the latter "dodging in and out," over some 500 lines.

Among Kaufman's contributions to this exchange are enough gems to make its three-buck price tag a major bargain—from small kinesthetic moments of embodied vision ("I will love you / in landscapes / of liquid stone . . . there will be frost, / when the great bell of space rings") to flashes of pure propositional power: "No trick of fate is played on / those who by indirection create / identified flying objects / of themselves, and live / aloft forever, / abstract / expressionism, non-objective . . . suffering causes love, / love causes suffering, / the death of / birds is sad, / love survives it . . . two of us becoming / the place we are in, / become superior beings / from another planet, / where our souls and / bodies meet on the / eternal bed of flowers."

You take the Harvard anthology of contemporary American poetry; I'll take Bob Kaufman.

Selfless Attention

Left Out in the Rain is a kind of Snyder retrospective. Not that the poems here are familiar; they aren't. The 154 pieces in this volume, ranging from some impressive nature meditations done in the author's teenage years to one poem written in China in 1985, have never been published before.

Though new to us, they're not new in a chronological sense; from the last half-decade there are only a handful of poems (five to be exact). Whether this means Snyder has reserved other recent poems for different projects is anybody's guess. He provides no information as to his reasons for excluding this work from previous books, and his publisher isn't much more forthcoming on the point, enigmatically attributing the poems' nonappearance until now to "chance or design." That leaves a lot of room for surmise. Some of these pieces were obviously too slight to go into books, others evidently just didn't fit.

But before anyone jumps to the conclusion that this is back-of-the-drawer material—juvenilia and marginalia—it must be said first of all that there are many fine poems here; and second that this is one of Snyder's better books, perhaps the one that will afford the best glimpse yet of what now looks like a very coherent poetic career. A third claim could be made for the book: It provides the closest thing to an autobiography Snyder has given us yet. While this is true, it's also somewhat beside the point because, throughout this poet's life-narrative-

Review of *Left Out in the Rain: Poems 1947–1984* by Gary Snyder, *San Francisco Chronicle,* 1986.

in-verse, his attention remains steadily fixed on the world he finds himself in, rather than on himself.

That quality of selfless attention is crucial to Snyder's procedure as a poet. It's the key quality in even his earliest mature poems, like those written in Berkeley when he was doing Buddhist studies there in the mid-fifties—the William Carlos Williams-ish no-ideas-but-in-things "Plum petals falling . . ." (1954), or the gemlike "The Rainy Season" (1955), whose "diamond-point" clarity makes it read almost like an illustration out of Ezra Pound's *ABC of Reading*.

Indeed, all the factors that converged to form Snyder's adult style—not only the influence of Williams, Pound and the Chinese and Japanese classics, but his own very unliterary and inquisitive character—have that one thing in common: a quality of caring attention to the world. It's something his Buddhism helped refine, as did his endless adventuring in nature, whether on the job (as logger, lookout, seaman) or roughing it with rucksack in the Cascades, the Sawtooths or the Sierra.

Attention, in fact, is the subject of what might be the best poem in the book, a 1960 piece called "Crash," written in Kyoto, where the poet lived for a number of years in the fifties and sixties. This poem dramatizes the tensions that Snyder (model Buddhist though he was) seems to have experienced as an American living in Japan. Here the confrontation is almost allegorically dramatic, a cross-cultural collision that occurs when the motorcycle-mounted poet runs over a slow-moving Japanese bicyclist. "Where was my mind," the shaken Snyder asks himself. "Later at the temple," he gets his reply: "I saw my inattention, / Tiny moment in the thread, / Was where the whole world could have turned / And gone another way." A moment's distraction, he's suggesting, can undo lifetimes; the hair-thin variance that separates routine event from catastrophe is no more or less than the quality of the mind's attention.

Poetry, the highest intensity of attention, is projected here as primary value. Snyder's metaphor for this is contained in a 1975 poem title, "Poetry Is the Eagle of Experience." (In his figure, poetry soars above "All the little mice of writing letters, / Sorting papers, / And the rabbits of getting in wood, / The big

Buck of a lecture in town.") What he has been after all along is nothing less than "High Quality Information" (as another poem title has it) and this book is a record of "A life spent seeking it / Like a worm in the earth, / Like a hawk."

Those empty back places beyond the side roads that hold so much appeal for Snyder are the places where that kind of information is still waiting to be found. The gods of the place, the ghosts of the past, the life of the present and the hope of the future—they're all still there, he tells us, waiting. "The Route," a small 1969 piece about the American experience, accents this, making it clear that for Snyder the earnest hope of a fruitful frontier continually flickers: "We didn't go so much to the south / As to the west. / Following the hills. / Beating the bad / Greeting the good." "History is made of mistakes," perhaps, but this poet always trusts that there remains "Lots of play / in the way things work, / in the way things are" ("Lots of Play").

"The Other Side of the Coin" (another poem title here) is civilization as it now exists, out there beyond Snyder's Sierra foothill homestead. Government planes buzz the pot farmers who are his neighbors; a restaurant sign proclaiming "No Shoes No Shirt No Service" reminds him that Shiva, the Bushmen, the Paiutes and the queens of Crete wouldn't be welcome. The degree of present danger to the planet and its living inhabitants, objects of the poet's attention and compassion, is hinted at in a prophetic poem called "Bomb Test" (1956): "The fish float belly-up, for real— / uranium in the whites / of their eyes . . ." A world so poisonously "clean" that it won't have room for poets or trees—that's the nightmare image that chases Gary Snyder off the freeway, back into the woods. His best reply to it comes in another 1969 poem, "Then," which predicts that in the future, "When everybody in the world has a car . . . they'll . . . dream of the days when men were poor and dirty— / it was great — / beggars, the wine-red saris / of outcaste Indian girls / lean hunger in the rain / —we were / alive then."

Bias for the Microcosmic

In one of Carl Rakosi's poems, L. S. Leakey, the anthropologist, is "holding / the skull / of Zinjanthropus, / 1,500,000 years / in his hand" ("The Response to Hamlet"). Rakosi's poems in this book date back *not quite* to the Pleistocene—but at least to the 1920s and the Objectivist movement, an early modernist way station that quietly closed down after its better-known travelers had passed through. (Among the other poets in Ezra Pound's *Objectivist Anthology* were George Oppen, Mina Loy, Charles Reznikoff, Marianne Moore, Louis Zukofsky and William Carlos Williams.)

Only Rakosi, who has been a San Francisco resident in recent years, remains to tell the tale, and his *Collected Poems* is now in our hands to do that for him.

The most immediate characteristics of Rakosi's voice are a flat plain tone, conveying a remarkable clarity and honesty, and a distinction in the choice of words, the pungent diction of a lover of American English: "Topaz and dandelion, / yes, / and crow's foot / (that's an odd one) / and quince . . ." ("Nature of Yellow"); "little river steamer from the tariff frontiers / . . . carries kilderkin imperial kegs and stingo firkins" ("Ships").

From a love of words to a love of things is the short but demanding leap that Rakosi makes in poem after poem, whether writing of a house in New Hampshire ("The maple fits upon the joist like a flower"), a sea animal ("Saltflush lobster / bull encrusted swims / backward from the rock") or a

Review of *The Collected Poems of Carl Rakosi, San Francisco Chronicle*, 1987.

nasturtium ("petals alight: / 20 watts of tangerine / shaded by green / leaf / a meticulous parasol / by Hokusai"). Such lines are small declarations of devotion to the literal, like flags announcing an allegiance beyond choice: "I mean to penetrate the particular / the way an owl waits for a kangaroo rat / and the photomicrograph beholds / the hairy pappus / of a dandelion" ("I Mean to Penetrate the Particular").

His bias for the microcosmic things of this world unites Rakosi with certain Chinese and Japanese poets, with the Frenchman Francis Ponge, and with his erstwhile fellow objectivists such as Moore and Williams. But the special poised tone, wavering precariously between sadness and whimsy, resignation and enthusiasm, makes his voice a unique one. Few other poets' specifications have been this precise.

> On the eighth thousandth magnification
> the chromosome of the Chironomus fly
> stirred its microscopic nebulae into
> the figure of a Greek Orthodox cross.
>
> ("The Romantic Eye")

Yet precision is not the whole story with Rakosi. His accuracy has, always, an undertone of praise that recalls us to his Hebraic recognition of a substantial world infused and transfigured by rays of the divine:

> Matter,
> with this look
> I wed thee
> and become
> thy very
> attribute.
> I shall be
> thy faithful
> spouse,
> true
> to thy
> nature,
> for I love
> thee

    more than Dürer
    loved
    a seaweed.

("The Vow")

Carl Rakosi's work is perhaps the best illustration of Goethe's dictum that modern poetry is an *art of occasions*. The bounds of his gift are outlined in a poem of self-limitation typically Rakosian in its candor: "As soon as I know its compass / I can write the poem. / If my suspicions were more grandiose / and I had the bile of a prophet / or could space myself out / on high metaphors / I could go long distances" ("As Soon As I Know Its Compass").

Though Rakosi has always left the big gestures to others, his *Collected* reminds us of poetry's ancient way of packing many of its best moments into its smallest spaces.

Romantic with a Cause

Ed Sanders's personal history spans a dozen mini-careers, from classics scholar to mystic-militant peace-and-love activist, from investigative reporter to rock 'n' roll star, from bohemian publisher and bookstore entrepreneur to utopian environmentalist and consumer advocate. He has fought Goliath-size adversaries from the Pentagon to the telephone company, and though he hasn't come out on top every time, the running score of his dauntless meta-political battle-against-big-odds is accurately summed up in the title of the 1984 reunion album issued by his on-again, off-again rock group, the Fugs: *Refuse to Be Burnt Out.*

The details of Sanders's initial Thoreauvian exercise in civil disobedience are etched in his first important work in verse, the 1961 *Poem from Jail*—still a pacifist classic, and properly given the lead-off position in this collection.

The poem documents the events of August 8, 1961, when the Polaris nuclear submarine Ethan Allen was commissioned at New London, Connecticut. At the time, Sanders was a twenty-one-year-old student of ancient languages; he'd come from Missouri to NYU to study nuclear physics in preparation for joining the national space program, but in college had found himself derailed into poetry and political radicalism.

On that day at New London he donned his custard-colored swimming suit with an Eye of Horus inked upon the front pocket, dove into the chilly water and headed for the missile-sub in "the fastest crawl in pacifist history." For this attempt to

Review of *Thirsting for Peace in a Raging Century: Poems by Edward Sanders 1960–1985, San Francisco Chronicle,* 1987.

block the submarine commissioning, Sanders wound up in a prison cell, where he wrote *Poem from Jail* in adapted Greek meters on a "scroll of toilet paper."

> Redeem Zion!
> Stomp up over
> the Mountain!
> To live as "beatific
> Spirits welded
> Together,"
> To live with
> a fierce pacifism,
> To love in haste,
> as a beetle entering bark,
> To dance with
> flaming mane . . .

The ecstatic rapture ("Tremble drama") life-celebration, death-defiance and serio-comic neologistic invention in *Poem from Jail* lay down the major chord of Sanders's work to come. Within a few years the future his poem had prophesied—of a "Now culture . . . balling its / way toward . . . pluperfection"—was something Sanders was working furiously to enact.

To a degree beyond any of his idols in poetry, even Allen Ginsberg, Sanders was a child of the media age, and his "total assault on the culture" (as he was fond of calling it) immediately took as many forms as modern technological society could provide. He opened the Peace Eye bookstore on New York's Lower East Side, inaugurated *Fuck You, a Magazine of the Arts,* made two wild pornographic movies and organized his satirical rock ensemble, the Fugs.

After the 1968 debacle of the Chicago convention, Sanders took a hard look at the seamy side of the "now culture" and retreated to a rural hideaway in Woodstock. There his "assault" gradually changed form and focus; he wrote novels and became a "data-freak," marshalling his "investigative poetics" to ecological and environmental projects, antinuclear and democratic consumer-activist campaigns. In recent years Sanders has been busy inventing space-age musical instruments to mobilize new politico-satirical rock operas. He has revived the Fugs and is touring again.

Throughout all this his reputation as social crusader has perhaps obscured his achievement as poet. For all its merit as a linguistic reflection of its times, the concerns of his poetry are far less specifically historical than cosmic and mythic.

Sanders's poems benefit by his long studies in Greek poetics and Egyptian hicroglyphs. This poet has actually learned not only from Pound, Williams and Ginsberg but from Sappho and Archilochus, Homer and Hesiod and the Book of the Dead. An exemplary instance of the harmonious wedding of passion and scholarship is his adaptation of a famous Sapphic lyric:

> I see a dizzy nothing,
> my ears ring with noise,
> the sweat runs down
> upon me, and a trembling
> that I can not stop
> seizes me limb and loin,
> o I am greener than grass, and
> death seems so near . . .
> ("Sappho's Poem Beginning 'Phainetai Moi' ")

But this is a poet whose traditional sources and devices are not limited to the ancient classics. Sanders's belief in the eternity of souls, in the redemptive power of love and in the relief of human suffering through libertarian behavior allies him with ideological Romantics from Shelley onward ("the concept of concerted love-zap assumed the Shelleyan belief that the *will* of the species can overcome evil," he writes in a note to one poem).

And his allegiance to the methodological principle of data-gathering and enlightened intelligence activity are his legacy from the eighteenth- and nineteenth-century champions of factual research. He aims, as he's said, to resurrect that investigative spirit in a new "Z-D Generation," founded on the examples of Zola and Diderot. These aims have consistently and increasingly informed his poems.

For 15-thousand years
the plutonium
in the smoke detector
lay in the Woodstock dump
till the day
the grade-blader scraped it out
& smashed it to chiplets
the chipmunk pulled
to the pouch of his cheeks
& during
the next 200
               years
it caused
         6 cancers
in a skunk
a crow a deer
a dog   a dog
and Johnny McQuaife

                              ("The Chain")

Thirsting for Peace in a Raging Century is a book long over-due. It restores Ed Sanders to his rightful place at the fore-front of the poetry of his time, and reminds us that spending one's days in active pursuit of the betterment of all life on the planet isn't necessarily antithetical to the creation of first-rate writing.

Doing Hard Time for Poetry

Courage and *poetry* are terms we're not used to associating, unless it's to say that it takes the former to sit through the latter. Very few of our poets are forced to go to jail for their writings (not that there aren't some likely candidates). And if they were, how many of them, do you suppose, would pass the time inscribing verses on soap bars with sharpened matchsticks, or committing 300 poems, composed in this manner, to memory?

We're talking about cultural differences, of course: This is the "free world," not the world of gulags and *samizdat*. Even for that other world, however, the achievement of Soviet poet Irina Ratushinskaya is a remarkable one. The poems of this avatar of Mandelstam, Akhmatova and Tsvetaeva are an inspiring reminder of the miraculous power of spirit to survive and overcome the most monolithically stifling and hopeless of contexts.

A young teacher of physics and mathematics in Odessa, then later in Kiev, Ratushinskaya ran into trouble with the KGB for her participation in human rights activities and for her irritating insistence on producing nonideological poetry. Arrested in 1982, she was sentenced the following March—on the day after her twenty-ninth birthday—to a twelve-year term, the first seven years of it to be served in a "corrective labor camp" in primitive swamp country 300 miles southeast

Review of *Beyond the Limit* by Irina Ratushinskaya, translated by Frances Padorr Brent and Carol J. Avins, *San Francisco Chronicle*, 1987.

of Moscow. (This sentence was the harshest imposed on a woman political prisoner since the death of Josef Stalin.)

There Ratushinskaya experienced deprivations familiar to readers of labor camp literature. Her earlier work in preparing clandestine photographic editions of Solzhenitsyn's books, she says, had prepared her for her ordeal, and through it all she refused offers of clemency in return for collaboration with the KGB. Unexpectedly released as a "gift to the West" on the eve of the 1986 Reykjavik Summit, she emigrated with her husband, a dissident physicist, to this country.

Beyond the Limit is a cycle of forty-seven poems written during the first years of Ratushinskaya's term in the "strict regime" camp. Many of the poems were composed in an unheated isolation cell to which she'd been consigned after several hunger strikes. Given all that, it's not surprising that separation, distance, loneliness and longing are key themes in the poems. More surprising is the absence of hysteria or self-pity.

The poems repeatedly lift off into levels of wit and imagination—and sometimes an almost playful lightness—that suggest a strength being drawn from somewhere beyond the physical dimensions of the bleak captivity from which they proceed. They are political only in the sense of their overwhelming commitment to life. Many seem to begin in the prisoner's lowest moments ("a cracking of bones—just at the point of breaking"), and then to ascend, gradually, with small hopeful leaps ("Quiet angel takes wing. Fate will twist matters for us—may we only survive!").

My only reservation about this bilingual edition concerns the quality of the translation, which occasionally wobbles in and out of rhetorical awkwardness (for example, in the deflating close of a poem ending "the hand's no longer a hand, and Virgo gives a laugh"). One can't help feeling such passages are like the frost on the isolation-cell window-glass that Ratushinskaya makes a key metaphor in one of her finest poems—a circumstantial distortion we don't so much overlook as gratefully see through.

That poem, like most in the cycle, is untitled and identified only by its compositional date—appropriately, since here as everywhere in *Beyond the Limit,* time is Ratushinskaya's phantom subject:

> I'll live through this, survive, and they'll ask me:
> how they beat my head on the prison cot,
> how it froze during the nights,
> how the first wisps of gray hair broke through.
> I'll smile and say some joke,
> wave away the shadow that comes quickly,
> and I'll honor the dry September
> that's become my second birth.
> And they'll ask: doesn't it hurt to remember?
> without being deceived by the lightness around?
> But names from the past burst in my memory—
> beautiful—like old weapons.
> And I'll tell about the best in all the world,
> the most tender, who don't break,
> how they accompanied us, how they went to torture,
> awaited letters from those they loved.
> And they'll ask: what helped us live,
> without letters or news—just walls
> and coldness in the cell, stupidity of official lies,
> nauseating promises for betrayal.
> And I'll tell about the first beauty which I saw in this
>   captivity:
> window in the frost! No spy holes, nor walls,
> nor grating—no long suffering—
> only bluish light in the smallest glass.
> Whirling pattern—you can't dream of anything more
>   enchanted!
> Look close, you'll see it begin to blossom even more:
> forests of thieves, fires, birds!
> and how many times there was coldness
> and how many windows glistened from that time on. But it
>   hasn't happened again,
> such violence of prism-ice,
> and why should it be mine—now,
> —and what have I done to deserve this holiday?
> Such a gift can happen only once.
> Perhaps one needs it only once.
>
> 30 November 1983

Traumatic Youth

At the beginning of his 1929 autobiography, *Goodbye to All That*, British poet Robert Graves took a playful swipe at what he called "biographical convention": "proper chaps have their formal geography, however little it may mean to them. They have birth certificates, passports, relatives, earliest recollections, and even, sometimes, degrees and publications and campaigns to itemize. . . ."

Graves's own memoir of his early years was distinctly *unconventional*, the terrain it charted highly personal. Now, more than a half-century later, his nephew, biographer Richard Perceval Graves (who has previously written lives of T. E. Lawrence, A. E. Housman and the Powys brothers), has undertaken to redraw the map of those years, restoring some of their "formal geography."

The Assault Heroic covers the same ground as *Goodbye to All That,* but from a different angle. Understandably, Graves the poet was more interested in examining the growth of his mind and emotions than in getting the facts straight. By contrast, his nephew the biographer carefully dates and documents external events. But for the life of the inner man, Richard Graves has had to borrow from the best source on that subject—his uncle's own memoir. He frequently quotes from *Goodbye,* as well as from Graves's letters, both indispensable sources on the conflicted inner life of his difficult subject.

But comparing *Goodbye* with the present book is almost like comparing fiction with fact. What *The Assault Heroic* lacks in

---

Review of *Robert Graves: The Assault Heroic 1895–1926* by Perceval Graves, *San Francisco Chronicle*, 1987.

dramatic intensity it makes up for in breadth of information and balance of judgment. Richard Graves draws heavily on heretofore unseen family papers (especially the diaries of Robert Graves's father, the unpublished memoirs of his mother and an incomplete biographical study written by his younger brother John). Robert Graves's own highly subjective self-portrait of the artist as a young man now has its perfect complement: a portrait from the point of view of those who knew him best, his close family.

After devoting five chapters to his subject's antecedents (Robert Von Ranke Graves is baptized on page 28), the biographer informs us that Graves inherited his "iron constitution" and "rather narrow idealism" from his German-born mother's side of the family, while getting "a good humor, a bad business sense, a great love of words . . . enormous pride [and] sensitivity" from his Irish father's side. He points out that the Graves clan gave high value to tradition and family history, and suggests that growing up in such a family endowed Robert with his own passion for history, later put to use in such novels as *I, Claudius*.

Robert Graves's family was large, even by Victorian-bourgeois standards: There were nine other children in the household, five of them from his father's first marriage. All the Graves children were under great pressure from their parents to succeed in life; as Richard Graves shows, many of them suffered emotional debilitation because of it. Driven by the ambition of his father, an Inspector of Schools and composer of light ballads, and by the idealism of his mother, a would-be missionary nurse who gave up her "vocation" for marriage, young Robert began inventing poetry at a very early age (his nephew/biographer quotes some ingenious rhymed verses dictated by the budding poet at age three).

For Graves, poetry soon became an escape from life's harsher moments. And there were many such moments to endure during the twelve years he spent as a boarder in a succession of rigorous prep schools. In *Goodbye to All That* he vividly recounted the miseries of those years: the raggings to which school bullies subjected him because of his German ancestry; his prudish shock when confronted with the other boys' "rude" sexual practices; the idealized love he felt for a boy three years his junior. Summarizing this same material, Richard brings to it a cooler, more detached perspective. He quotes, for example, Robert's schoolmates, who viewed these events quite differently, finding young Graves "priggish" and "uncompanionable."

In the summer of 1914, the nineteen-year-old Graves left Charterhouse School, bound for Oxford. A month later, the world-as-known collapsed around him: War broke out. His pacifist sentiments notwithstanding, the young poet volunteered for the Royal Welch Fusiliers, believing, as he wrote to a friend, that France was "the only place for a gentleman now." By May 1915 he had joined the other "gentlemen" at the front.

The horrors of trench warfare, evoked with such visceral immediacy in *Goodbye to All That,* are somewhat distanced and toned down in *The Assault Heroic. Goodbye*'s graphic description of a fellow soldier unwrapping his blanket only to discover rats fighting over a severed hand, for example, is here reduced to one phrase: "a plague of rats."

The biographer does, however, give us more detail about Graves's participation in the disastrous September 1915 Battle of Loos, where a release of poison gas, meant for the enemy, drifted back instead to choke British troops. And he covers blow-by-blow the drawn-out July 1916 Battle of the Somme, where Graves, seriously wounded by a shell blast, was taken for dead and reported "killed in action." These traumatic incidents, which plagued the shell-shocked veteran for years afterwards, are harrowing even in secondhand account.

It's in his coverage of the postwar years that Richard Graves makes his most significant contribution. He provides a sympathetic rendering of Graves's increasingly difficult marriage to the feminist painter Nancy Nicholson (the couple had four children in close succession, lost money in impractical farming and shopkeeping schemes and frequently had to borrow from friends and family). He also relates interesting anecdotes about Graves's literary associates (notably Siegfried Sassoon, T. E. Lawrence, Thomas Hardy, Edith Sitwell, Virginia Woolf, John Masefield and Laura Riding) and traces Graves's poetic development from a writer of fairly conventional war poetry and pastoral verse to the author of brooding philosophical meditations reflecting a growing interest in magic, myth, "associative" thought and psychoanalysis.

This dense book ends on a note of suspense: "Whether Robert would remain an interesting minor poet or whether he would achieve something more, must have seemed an open question in January 1926 . . ." Of course literary history has long since supplied the answer; but we can still look forward with some anticipation to the next installment of Richard Perceval Graves's multi-volume project.

Personal Handling

Trained as a painter, Marsden Hartley made a name for himself in his early thirties with his first one-man show at Alfred Stieglitz's legendary 291 Gallery in 1908.

With other members of Stieglitz's 291 group, such as Arthur Dove and John Marin, Hartley joined the first wave of American modernists in the arts, beginning a career whose wanderings took him to Paris, the south of France, Berlin and Mexico before finally settling in his native Maine in the 1930s.

Throughout this long and varied career as a visual artist, Hartley pursued a second calling with equal dedication, if not with equal professional success. This was poetry, to which he devoted half his working hours, typically spending his mornings with pen and paper and his afternoons—when he found the light more conducive to painting—with brush and canvas.

Though only three collections of Hartley's verse appeared during his life, he was on personal terms with the most forward literary figures of his time: Ezra Pound, Gertrude Stein, Hart Crane, Marianne Moore, William Carlos Williams. It was Hartley, for example, who introduced Williams to Robert McAlmon, thus providing a spark for the landmark magazine, *Contact.*

This constellation of literary associations has led to a bracketing of Hartley's work with that of his modernist colleagues, albeit as a minor figure. Although such a categorical description may indeed do justice to his earlier poems, which take their small place in the history of international experi-

---

Review of *The Collected Poems of Marsden Hartley 1904–1943*, edited by Gail R. Scott, *San Francisco Chronicle,* 1987.

mentalism, it misses the point of his best work, those pieces from his final years, when he had returned not only to the Down-East landscapes of his childhood but to a rough-hewn, close-to-hand, "eye with brain in it" aesthetic:

"Personal handling counts for more than personal confession. We are the most original when we are like life," Hartley wrote in *The Business of Poetry*. "Nature is always variable. To have an eye with brain in it—that is, or rather would be, the poetic millennium."

This agenda approximated the democratic aims of his real poetic predecessor, Walt Whitman, much more closely than it did those of his erstwhile literary-revolutionary friends.

These are poems whose "personal handling" shows Hartley to be a true American primitive in poetry; they are perhaps less "ambitious" than what remains of his internationalist period in writing, but at the same time more interesting and certainly far more readable.

They remind us that Hartley went at poetry without formal training ("all my poems are written first draft and left," he confessed to McAlmon in 1941); that his existence was a lonely and rootless one, from the early death of his mother through his ordeal of living as a homosexual in an age when no support community was easily available; and that his true gift in poetry was finally one of eye and hand, not of grand scheme or concept.

Hartley's preoccupation with the concrete and local, the "variable" in "Nature," can be seen in many short pieces such as "Serving the Curve" ("Serving the curve of this coast / the wind lazes along, winding / itself among the perched starlings / on the weather vane of the defunct / church . . .").

Such poems convey Hartley's regional sensibility, his mastery of place. They are fine things. But here and there he goes further, investing the local with active senses of the moral and personal, fully capturing a life:

> When the surf licking with its tongue
> these volcanic personal shapes, which we
> defining for ourselves as rocks, accept

them as such, at its feverish incoming—
isn't it too, in its way, something like
the plain image of life—
those restless entities disturbing solid
substances with a curious, irrelevant, common fret—
And, like so many simple looking elements, when
they seem the most playful, it is then that
they are most dangerous . . .

This is from "Indian Point," a poem in which one finds the best of a poet whose quality as an "American original" here reaches its home.

Versatile and Doomed

Poet, cultural critic, novelist, story-writer, Abstract Expressionist painter, jazz musician, composer, filmmaker—Weldon Kees accurately termed himself "the most versatile artist now working in America." That was in 1955 when, at forty-one, Kees had—as he told a correspondent—"so many damned irons in the fire it looks like branding time at the old Bar Z."

Along the trail that led Kees from Beatrice, Nebraska, to the Bay Area there were very few dull moments. After an arts apprenticeship in Denver he made his way in the early 1940s to New York, where, parlaying a promising poetic talent with highly developed social skills, he quickly shouldered his way into the Manhattan literary scene, befriending Edmund Wilson, Allen Tate and the *Partisan Review* crowd.

Before long he'd also taken up painting, succeeded Clement Greenberg as art critic of *The Nation,* and managed to nudge his own work—intelligent and derivative—onto gallery walls side-by-side with the Pollacks and de Koonings.

By 1950 the dapper, slightly pushy kid from the plains had not only crashed but conquered Manhattan's highly exclusive art party. Restlessly he moved West, to Berkeley and then San Francisco.

Here his energies continued to flourish and expand. He involved himself with local poets (like Kenneth Rexroth) and painters (like Hassell Smith and Douglas MacAgy), and with the fifties jazz revival (he played piano with Turk Murphy, and initiated a minor career as a songwriter). The archetypal

Review of *Weldon Kees and the Midcentury Generation: Letters, 1935–1955,* edited by Robert E. Knoll, *San Francisco Chronicle,* 1987.

early multimedia man, Kees made films, worked briefly at KPFA, and generally stretched his talent as far—and also, perhaps, as thin—as possible; yet still found time to cultivate his first and best gift, the writing of poetry, culminating in the volume *Poems 1947–1954*, issued by San Francisco's master fine-printer Adrian Wilson.

But beneath the froth of activity, Kees was by this time a desperate man, compulsive, manic-depressive, isolated after the breakdown of his wife and the breakup of his marriage. At work on a book about nonverbal communication, he was nonetheless insufficiently adept at communication to signal his condition to friends (he would have considered such "unburdening" to be "in bad taste," one recalls).

On June 1, 1955, Kees's abandoned car was found near the Golden Gate Bridge, the last trace of his apparent suicide. It was a death anticipated in the deep-water obsessions of his poetry:

> Nothing will be the same as it once was,
> I tell myself.—It's dark here on the peak, and keeps on get-
> ting darker.
> It seems I am experiencing a kind of ecstasy.
> Was it sunlight on the waves that day? The night comes down.
> And now the water seems remote, unreal, and perhaps it is.
> ("A Distance from the Sea")

Scholar Robert E. Knoll here edits Kees's letters—witty, talky, newsy, charming, ironic, catty, full of literary-artistic gossip and name-dropping—and gives useful informational linkages that chronicle the career of this talented, unstable bit player in the mid-century arts game on both coasts: A figure whose marginal role provided him material for sharp epistolary commentary but not the judgment or objectivity that survival would have required.

Still Sounding

The poet H.D., or Hilda Doolittle (1886–1961), left a Philadel-
phia suburb a few years before the First World War to become a
brief part of literary history in Europe, a modernist alongside
her literary promoter Ezra Pound, with whom she'd once had a
schoolgirl fling. Fresh off the boat in London, she was tagged
by Pound an "Imagiste." The tag stuck, though the auratic,
hieratic priestess's voice of H.D.'s writing never quite harmo-
nized with the less elevated strains of modernist poetic associates like Pound. Closer in spirit to H.D.'s passionate intensities
("somewhat fine-wrought," she termed her poetic persona in
one verse, "fiery tempered, delicate, over-passionate steel")
was D. H. Lawrence, with whom she shared a strong personal
affinity. But where H.D. and Lawrence ultimately diverged was
over the issue of "the man-pulse," that pseudo-force Lawrence
worshiped and H.D. regarded as a mere "trick" employed by
men to hoodwink and subdue women, and themselves.

Editor Louis Martz, in his introduction to the timely and
useful *Selected Poems,* is surely correct in stressing H.D.'s isolation. If, as Martz suggests, Pound and Lawrence merely
joined British poet-husband Richard Aldington in a general
male failure to understand her, then it's equally true H.D.
eventually made the most of her passionate autonomy in life
and poetry. "At least I have the flowers of myself," she was

Review of *H.D.: Selected Poems,* edited by Louis Martz; *The Collected
Poems of William Carlos Williams: Volume II, 1939–1962,* edited by Christopher MacGowan; and *The Collected Poetry of Robinson Jeffers: Volume I,
1920–1928,* edited by Tim Hunt, *San Francisco Chronicle,* 1988.

proposing as early as the 1917 poem "Eurydice," "and my thoughts, no god / can take that."

In her mature poetry she first adopted the neo-Greek classic mask of Sappho, writing in a fragmentary, ecstatic, entranced voice caught up in the mystery and "fright of beauty," making poems as durable, enclosed and vibrant with implication as archaic carvings.

During years of personal anguish and despair after the War, a time of lonely, refining silence, her sexual identity emerged with new and challenging clarity. "Is there none left," she asked in the 1924 poem "Cassandra," "can equal me / in ecstasy, desire?" A decade later, in a period of creative ebb and self-questioning over her bisexuality—"I had two lives separate," she summarized her case history in poetry—she underwent psychoanalytic treatment by Dr. Sigmund Freud, who reassured her she was a poet but told her she needed a man in her life to sustain her. "Angry with the old man / with his talk of the man-strength," H.D. responded with a vivid new burst of self-affirming, prophetic poetry ("It was he himself," she credited Freud in her poem of tribute to him, "who set me free to prophesy").

Announcing in the now-celebrated (and in some cases only lately published) "lost" poems of the thirties a redemptive return of the female principle to a spiritually distressed world, she did indeed take on the prophet's mantle in poetry, anticipating the spirit of the current feminist movement by a good half century. (Martz notes that the present-day women's struggle for liberty can be seen as in some respects an extension of "the essential struggle that lies deep within her poetry.") These poems are well represented here, as are the visionary meditative "Trilogy" written during the Second World War in London, and the late, great, Blake-like mytho-Biblical prophetic sequences of "Hermetic Definitions" and "Helen in Egypt," summoning a "magic greater than the trial of arms." H.D.'s is an intriguing Cassandra's voice beckoning us back across the clutter and business of the twentieth century to primordial mysteries.

Among the youthful H.D.'s first admirers was a University

of Pennsylvania medical school student named William Carlos Williams, who later recalled her in girlhood as possessing a "provocative indifference to rules and order," and an uneasy skittishness "found in wild animals at times." If it was that intuitive primal gift and uneasiness of H.D.'s which made her a poet, it was Williams's own eye for the vivid brilliance of nature manifesting itself in the human world that made *him* one. Much as has been made of the poet-doctor's initial vow to discover—and deliver—"no ideas but in things," the simple truth remains that it's the human understanding saturating all his mature writing which makes it so exceptional. This is made more clear than ever by *The Collected Poems*.

In these majestic poems, now painstakingly restored to original compositional states and attended by invaluable notes on text and biographical backdrop, that famous early vow can be seen for what it was: an expression in literary terms of an ingrained resistance to the abstract, the specious, everything that falsifies and exploits nature in persons and in the world. Its complement is an almost religious devotion to the actual shape of the moment, however joyous, painful, or plain.

> at the small end of an illness
> there was a picture
> probably Japanese
> which filled my eye
>
> an idiotic picture
> except it was all I recognized
> the wall lived for me in that picture
> I clung to it as a fly
> ("The World Contracted to a Recognizable Image")

All Williams's labor over the years to define the nature of his art by practicing it, his endless care and trouble over the fine points of the poem, now appear revealed in the solid beauty of his work's final coherence.

While contemporaries looked to pre-antiquity, to America's speech, or into their own souls for traces of the authentic, the notorious, self-professed "anti-modernist" Robinson Jeffers turned away from the human world altogether, assuming the eternal planet-consciousness of rocks, kelp and buzzards. His long-lined, doomy verse epistles against civilization were controversial in their day, but time, and a chronically combative, nest-fouling human race, have vindicated Jeffers as a cosmic philosopher, proving him less cranky than accurate in his dark forecasting of an encroaching "catastrophic time." His reply in its face is his defiant identification with the life force of nature that looms and soars in his poetry.

The developing poetic stages of that starkly grand cosmic view are now being laid bare in an ambitious, definitive four-volume standard edition inaugurated with *The Collected Poetry of Robinson Jeffers: Volume 1, 1920–1928*. The Stanford edition begun herein will present in its first three volumes all Jeffers's published poems chronologically, from 1920 through 1963, establishing what is projected by its editor as a "Jeffers canon," with a fourth volume reserved for "apprentice work" (1912–1919), uncompleted manuscript poems, and basic textual apparatus.

No mention is made of notes, and while it's true that over-annotating—the attempt to explicate through footnotes—can spoil the implication-potential of verse, it's also true that some detailed bio-history of the poems themselves might provide a useful flashlight for following the poet into all those dark cosmic spaces. Jeffers's poems—here moving from the early collection *Tamar,* which established his reputation in 1923, to *Cawdor* (1928)—are magnificent on their own, but for sixty dollars, the buyer deserves all the illumination he or she can get.

Still, no review of such poetry can end on a quibble. In this first volume, Jeffers's enduring themes of man's doom and nature's power emerge in poems that are sentinels for the century: "Phenomena," "Shine, Perishing Republic," "Continent's End," "Point Joe," "Hurt Hawks." As America plunged into the affluence of the Jazz Age—"While this America settles in the mould of its vulgarity, heavily thickening to empire"—Jeffers stared across history into the geological death of the continent, a lone voice intoning natural truths against the thin hopefulness of Progress.

The long migrations meet across you and it is nothing to you,
   you have forgotten us, mother.
You were much younger when we crawled out of the womb
   and lay in the sun's eye on the tideline.

It was long and long ago; we have grown proud since then
   and you have grown bitter; life retains
Your mobile soft unquiet strength; and envies hardness, the
   insolent quietness of stone.

The tides are in our veins, we still mirror the stars, life is your
   child, but there is in me
Older and harder than life and more impartial, the eye that
   watched before there was an ocean.

("Continent's End")

Dark Glory

The long, rolling, wave-crashing-on-rock cadences of the verse in this second volume of the massive Stanford *Collected Poetry* expresses Robinson Jeffers's fully mature vision at mid-career. The poems cover the years 1928 to 1938, or by bibliographic chronology the stretch between *Dear Judas* (published in 1929) and *Such Counsels You Gave Me* (1937). They were composed mostly in the isolation and wildness of the poet's rough-hewn granite retreat on a rocky bluff above Carmel Bay, but also in the outriding solitudes of his occasional getaway travels.

The latter, judging by the poems' evidence, were not so much holidays in the routine sense as instinctive pilgrimages to those "living rocks" whose "grave, earnest, not passive . . . energies" Jeffers sought to tap as other vacationers might pursue sunshine or healing waters.

The "Descent to the Dead" sequence here, commemorating a trip to the British Isles, is saturated with bleak ruminations on megalithic emblems of the poet's Scotch-Irish genetic origins. The Celtic and pre-Celtic cairns and quarries, cromlechs and dolmens left behind by races of men who'd once "died bloodily" reminded Jeffers that "death's nothing, and life . . . is nothing either." And yet—according to the Jeffers stoic-pessimist philosophy—"How beautiful are both these nothings."

While abroad the poet wandered highland burial mounds, pondered the stones over Shakespeare's grave, plotted an inscription for his own grave marker ("I am not dead, I have

Review of *The Collected Poetry of Robinson Jeffers: Volume II, 1928–1938*, edited by Tim Hunt, *San Francisco Chronicle*, 1989.

only become inhuman"), and paused to compose a gloomy little elegy for the French wartime premier Clemenceau, voiced by those driven by the leader's decisions to death in battle "like flies on a fire": "We don't say it was wrong. / We don't say it was right. / These heavy choices are less than verbal, down here, to us dead."

Other travels of the period took the poet several times to the Taos pueblo, where his observation of fellow spectators at a corn dance gave rise to one of his finest poems, "New Mexican Mountain." It staged a dominant Jeffers theme, the alienation of contemporary people from a vivid natural cosmos. "I don't think industrial civilization is worth the distortion of human nature, and the meanness and loss of contact with the earth, that it entails," he said in a letter to a friend around this time.

The city-bred tourists of his poem, greedy, restless "pilgrims from the vacuum . . . anxious to be human again," are a purely negative force, capable only of sucking dry the ancient ritual before them. Transformed into a diverting spectacle, "The Indians are emptied, / And certainly there was never religion enough, nor beauty nor poetry here . . . to fill Americans." The poem's final verse, Jeffers's gesture of passionate identification with all that remains after this sad draining of value, brings us back once more to that "living rock," the cosmic disinterestedness beyond death to which all his poetry returns. "Apparently only myself and the strong / Tribal drum, and the rock head of Taos mountain, remember that civilization is a transient sickness."

Jeffers's grand, shimmering reflections of the wild and enduring natural beauties of the California coastal environment are well known to all readers of poetry, and are to be rediscovered here in abundance. So also are his haunting prophecies of civilization's ruin, which seem far nearer to realization today than when he first bleakly hymned them—a grim neo-Calvinist Cassandra making out "far fires and dim degradation" in store for the "Perishing Republic" around him.

This central volume of the *Collected* has a nobility and dignity that must be approached and taken in slowly and in all its fullness, from the opening poem's first hintings at a post-human "dark glory . . . after the inquisitive animal's / Amusements are quiet," to the final resounding echoes of the last one, "Theory of Truth," an implicitly religious anticipation of ultimate redemption to be found in the supra-human totality of the universe, once "the mind has turned its love from itself and man, from parts to the whole."

My Sin

William Everson, also known as Brother Antoninus, the poetry-writing Dominican lay brother who at the height of his fame in the 1960s was dubbed by *Time* magazine "the Beat Friar," is the subject of this workmanlike but at times frustrating first biography by Lee Bartlett, an academic scholar and Everson's bibliographer.

Poets' lives, as John Keats once suggested, are often allegories. The obvious parable in Everson's life, as exhibited in Bartlett's version, is that old familiar oedipal tale of incestuous love and guilt. "My mother was a goddess," Everson wrote at twenty-five, "and my father was an ogre." His biography can be read as a series of variations on that interlocking double theme: keeping the ogre down, capturing the goddess.

The importance of Everson's parents as more than just prologue to the story is a point made most vividly by the poet himself in autobiographical notes Bartlett attaches as an appendix. These notes, made during a time of psychic crisis when Everson was a Dominican lay brother in 1956, show how the poet's life has been overshadowed all along by the ominous dimensions of his parental projections.

The "ogre" father got his power from public displays of music and song. Everson senior was town bandmaster of the small San Joaquin Valley peach-farming community of Selma. People came from miles around to hear him sing and yodel, resplendent in the lights of the Saturday-night bandstand. He was a less admirable figure, however, in the eyes of his son, who

Review of *William Everson: The Life of Brother Antoninus* by Lee Bartlett, *San Francisco Chronicle,* 1988.

189

was locked from an early age in tense competition with him for the affections of the third player in the family romance.

As demanding as the bandmaster was, infant William soon began to draw his young mother's exclusive attention away to himself. The powerful attachment would never be severed. "The fate of man," Everson would one day write, "turns on the body of woman." For him, there was to be only one woman all along.

Young Everson lived at home until he was twenty-one, when the tension between father and son drove him to "get out and make a statement," as Everson later wrote.

He attended California State University at Fresno but dropped out after stumbling onto the poetry of Robinson Jeffers, which made his "whole inner world begin to tremble." He wrote his first poems and struck out to be a Jeffersian poet living and laboring in his rural California homeland.

He worked in a cannery as a pipe layer and in 1938, after an eight-year engagement, married his high school sweetheart—a strong "maternal" type, according to Bartlett. However, he was still too hung up on his real mother to make the marriage work. During the war years it simply petered out.

His mother's sudden death in 1940 brought out one of those themes from the allegory. The bereaved son, temporarily deranged by this "devastating blow," wept and beat upon her coffin. His father looked on, glaring. They never spoke again.

After a "mixed-up" period of three years, Everson found structure in an unlikely place: a Civilian Public Services camp for wartime conscientious objectors, where he was interned from 1943 to 1946. The Waldport, Oregon, camp offered a work regimen and male company, a welcome refuge from his confusions.

Pushing himself to overachieve, Everson became a significant participant in the artistic and political life of the camp, directing its Fine Arts Project and bringing out his pacifist *War Elegies* on the camp's alternative press.

In the postwar years, Everson came to the Bay Area to study fine press work and to join the thriving local poets' community, in which he already had significant supporters—

principally Robert Duncan, with whom he'd been corresponding for some time. He started his Equinox Press and was taken under the wing of Kenneth Rexroth, reigning power broker of the poetry scene, who billed him as an "autochthon" (a sort of hybrid of Walt Whitman, Abraham Lincoln and noble savage) and helped get his first major book out from New Directions. *The Residual Years* (1948) was a great success and won Everson a 1949 Guggenheim Fellowship.

The momentous conversion to Catholicism followed. It's a crucial point in the story, but Bartlett is evasive about the causes. Perhaps, we're told, it was all a great Jungian life "climacteric" or "perhaps more simply . . . he wanted to please a Catholic woman he was seeing regularly."

Here the biographer is holding back his important cards. In 1948, Everson married the San Francisco poet-artist Mary Fabilli, herself a recent Catholic convert, and, as other historians of the period have noted, it was under her influence that he made his own move to the church. (The couple separated the following year but remained legally wed until 1963.)

None of this is brought up in the body of Bartlett's book. A fine-print note in the acknowledgements at the back reveals that "No mention of . . . Mary Fabilli was made in deference to privacy."

But the biographer's "deference" is also a disservice to his readers, a piece of historical laundering that leaves a mystifying blank in his story. (The reader is left wondering, for example, if the same cause was responsible for the suppression of Everson's "spiritual autobiography," *Prodigious Thrust.)*

In any case, Bartlett relates that the poet-convert was soon shopping around for a religious order that would support his poetry and printing, finally settling on and being accepted by the relatively urbane Dominicans.

In 1951 he entered that order as a lay brother at St. Albert's College in Oakland, taking the name Brother Antoninus. "Captured by the great work archetype," as he put it, he embarked on an ambitious printing project. But his "intense need for perfection," "endless anxiety" and inability to bend his inner life to the yoke of "monastic psychology" colluded to blow the printing project "sky high"—and, before long, to bring Everson/Antoninus to the brink of a breakdown.

A year of "black depression" after dismally washing out of priesthood studies and returning to St. Albert's led to a psychic explosion in 1956. The brother poured his hang-ups onto paper for three solid days. The samples given here, such as one in which the monk brutally rips his mother's body into little pieces in order to "blot her out of his existence," are described by Bartlett as "repressed eroticism" but sound more like outright misogyny. The poet-monk was rendering justice unto Eve, who out of "penis-envy," he believed, had "castrated God in the garden of Eden by stealing His fruit."

The poetry, meanwhile, had "dried up." It was brought back to life in 1957 by the sudden appearance on the national horizon of Allen Ginsberg and the Beats, with whom the brother immediately felt able to identify. He wrote a Ginsbergian erotic poem, "River-Root" ("holy is the phallos"), a self-described attempt to "redeem" and "canonize" the "libidinous Beat energies."

The poetry of Antoninus appeared alongside "Howl" in the *Evergreen Review,* and he went on the road, beginning one of the most unusual—and successful—barnstorming poetry careers America has ever seen. His intense, lengthy, charismatic "encounters" played just about every major college and culture hall in the land.

Some of the more interesting moments in Bartlett's book concern this "going out into the world." It was quite a shock to everybody—the nation's Catholics, the order (which briefly revoked his shtick, the right to wear his robes in public) and, not least, the brother himself. He wanted it all—"wine, scotch, after-dinner drinks, everything"—but felt guilty about it, once going down on his knees in a posh restaurant to beg the Lord's forgiveness.

With fame came other forms of temptation. His "counseling" brought him into intimate contact with women and their "glorious" bodies. There was an affair with his "Mexican cross," Rose, an Arthur Murray Dance Studio instructor who kept priests' photos over her bed like "mooseheads."

Rose drove a convertible with the top down so that her

black hair could flow in the wind, wore tight dresses and My Sin perfume and never missed daily Mass. (She liked digging the aluminum spikes of altar-candle holders into her palms "to produce stigmata.") Everson wrote "The Rose of Solitude" to her: "I need a queen to serve," he said, "as St. John of the Cross needed St. Theresa."

There was always the danger of turning himself into an industry. He designed his own posters, wrote press releases about himself (signed "Virginia Spanner") and pressed on into the 1960s. During his triumphant 1961 Eastern tour, a Washington newspaper called him "God's own showman."

In December 1969, following a histrionic self-defrocking performed as the climax to a reading at the University of California at Davis, he left the order. Dominicans who had known and supported him for eighteen years were stunned. "To go on stage and remove his habit," one commented to Bartlett, made "many people feel used . . . It was just so unnecessary." Everson had revealed his plans to no one in the order but had prepared a press release, and the story made the front page of the *San Francisco Chronicle,* along with a murder at the Rolling Stones concert at Altamont.

The rest of Bartlett's book is postscript as the poet-printer, now a venerable eminence with a "girl bride" thirty-five years his junior, takes up and maintains through most of two decades a residential position at Kresge College, University of California at Santa Cruz.

Questions raised by Lee Bartlett's version of the Everson story remain to be answered, and the great vacuum in the middle created by the "deferential" removal of the poet's second wife is just one of them.

The relation between poetry, fame and public relations in America is highlighted here without critical judgment. So are this poet's use of women and of the church and the curious blend of spiritual submissiveness with violent phallicism in his work.

There are cases where it's fair to ask that a biographer call the bluff of his subject at least some of the time, and I think this is one of them. Failing that, the story feels not only less than fully told but oddly unedifying.

Pop Hooks

Elaine Equi makes an asset out of the interesting problem of being a poet of cosmopolitan talents stranded in that town of hog butchers and freight handlers, Chicago. Equi's two new collections reveal a sophisticated lyric-romantic sensibility obviously honed on New York, West Coast and international models. You'd think all that would set her at odds with the stormy, husky, brawling, notoriously unsubtle city which is her native place and subject. But Equi's clash of styles with her hometown is sidelong, not head-on: it ends up, after a few skirmishes, in collusion and alliance.

She gently chides Chicago's "Big Shoulders" masculinity, watching its men "dancing with tape measures, / Building things without any flowers," and comments ironically: "when they're done they'll want to hire some woman"; and admits sympathy with satanist Aleister Crowley, who on his one visit to the city "was bored" (Equi spies the ultramundane satanist's ghost lingering in her neighborhood, idly tampering with a geranium).

Challenged, though, she's quick to Chicago's defense with a full post-punk Dorothy-Parkerish kit of weapons: arched-eyebrow barbs, nervy, catchy hooks of pop-conscious metaphor, and double-meanings stitched in lighthandedly "as if doodled there / with invisible ink." In "Gypsy Show," as defiant response to all those urbane New York School poems about the bracing air of Manhattan, Equi delights in Chicago's own special weather, its winter blizzards reminding her of

---

Review of *The Corners of the Mouth* and *Accessories* by Elaine Equi, *San Francisco Chronicle*, 1988.

"some long forgotten cartoon character whose boa / sparks a fit of giggles . . . the snow / is always hot-blooded and tells / the fortune of whomever / it falls on." And though the Monsters of the Midway aren't mentioned, she boasts in her "Ode to Chicago" with tongue only halfway in cheek that "in my city / dinosaurs are not extinct . . . Nowhere else will you find rocks that perspire, / trees that grow hair." Elaine Equi may be the enlightened laureate Chicago's always deserved to make up for Carl Sandburg.

Flung toward Life

Alice Notley is a "New York poet" who grew up in the Mojave Desert. In this night-trip log-book of autobiographical self-reflections, all those personal "states" in between—from Florida, Illinois and Montana to love, dreams, and loss—are explored in poetic depth. Here, feeling her way in the dark through the aftermath of a beloved partner's death, Notley touches on every stage in the life of love and of the spirit, from the blissful peaks to the lowest of the bad valleys.

Up to now—with successful books like *When Spring Comes, Waltzing Matilda,* and *Margaret & Dusty*—Notley has been a poet notable for her flights of imaginative language, the kind of linguistic daring the eighteenth century called "fancy." But "ultimate things" like capital-*G* Grief are usually not viewed as the material of fancy. And this is a very different Notley, trained by suffering to make leaps into new musics and knowledge.

Free-associatively speedy as ever on the surface, here she lets a graver voice in under that nervy lyric one. Like a heart slowed by its burdens into occasionally missing a beat, her whole "sound" changes and deepens. "If Gertrude Stein had been able to write, she'd have written like that," Ed Dorn has said of *At Night the States,* "The aphasic lapses are brilliant." To my ear that skipped-rhythm, dropped-stitch quality, whether heart murmur or aphasia, makes Notley a more interesting poet than ever before.

With the death of the poet's lover come emotional states

Review of *At Night the States* by Alice Notley, *St. Mark's Poetry Project Newsletter,* 1988.

apparently continents apart. Poetry is the resolution of such vast contradictions—in this case, between a dissociated desolation and self-affirmation's exhilaration-beyond-loss: "this strange enrichment of the / spirit I feel though bereft." To the bereft one, constellations of sense and memory come back like floating islands of phantom pain, compressed into the moment-spaces of a word: "start," "weather," "song," "pine," "rose," "love," "wind," "dream," and "night."

> You're one of the faraway mapmakers now
> the scent of pine, then gone.
>
> > ("Poem")

> The star, desire,
> is herself
> skin shining
> in the
> black evergreen
> night
>
> > ("L'Etoile")

> Days go by but you
> stay secluded
> in your onyx jet walled villa on the
> dark side of
> our other Mother
>
> > ("Baby Lovely")

Stranded on this side of Death's deepest of night-states, the poet is left to pick up the pieces. "This person who sleeps in my bed," says Notley in a poem called "Sweetheart," has "slept there forever and yet / there was another." "And I will always be another / Unrecognizable to my mirror." The integration of the personality is a wavering sail in mortality's storms.

> I had a dream that I
> was marrying myself.
> Looking through a
> crystal; & from among the
> millions of refracted

>   brides she walked towards
>   me, white veil & dress & bouquet
> ("I Had a Dream That I")

> I dreamed that he came back secretly for a few days . . . there
> had been some delays . . . I asked him if he wished he could
> really stay & be living again. No, he said, he was tired of having
> to be so masculine, captain of a ship too tight, too small even.
> He wanted to be more feminine, quieter for a change . . .
> ("Vitamin Equals Cigarette")

Senses of self and other, female and male, are not easily pinned down in these states. Where an exploiter might address it as an emotional constant, Notley writes of bereavement as an archetype of bewildered variability. "The thousand arms of Love" entangle, but "the little self is canny," escaping into "the vehicle of only myself." And yet, and yet. "I could have stayed forever in your arms."

This is, finally, a redemptive book, and an uplifting one, for all its sorrows. The poems carry an Orphic quality of being flung toward life, and charmed, like "all / that courses through the / mirror that opens to song" ("Backyard").

The Knot of Fate

Octavio Paz, Mexico's leading poet and critic, has long been renowned for his depth of insight, stylistic elegance and wide learning, all of which are displayed in his erudite, stately, magisterial and free-ranging biography, *Sor Juana.*

This is a leisurely ramble through ideas, epochs and cultures, written in prose that's lucid and expository, lapidary and recondite, with the dense texturing of a Beethoven string quartet and the layered serial structure of a complex modern novel.

Proceeding not by linear narrative but in a series of richly interwoven essays, Paz builds a masterful reconstruction of his country's cultural past from three basic elements: history, life, work.

The history is that of seventeenth-century viceregal New Spain, caught in a gulf of paradox between the medieval worldview of the church and a new mannerist sensibility emanating from the mother country in this age of the Spanish baroque.

The life and work are those of one of this colonial society's most enigmatic and unusual products, a woman of exceptional creative and intellectual gifts, who was born into a world in which the expression of such gifts was reserved for males: Juana Ramirez de Asbaje, better known by her reli-

Review of *Sor Juana: Or, the Traps of Faith* by Octavio Paz, translated by Margaret Sayers Peden, and *A Sor Juana Anthology*, translated by Alan S. Trueblood, foreword by Octavio Paz, *San Francisco Chronicle*, 1988.

gious name in the Hieronymite order, Sor (or Sister) Juana Inés de la Cruz.

"Of the major poets of our hemisphere," Paz suggests in his prologue, "a number are women, Juana Inés de la Cruz, Emily Dickinson, Gabriela Mistral, Marianne Moore and Elizabeth Bishop.

"It is not hard to see that these five have several things in common, apart from their sex. All, for example, were unmarried and all lived somewhat at the fringes of their time and world, vitally conscious of their singularity both as women and as poets. Nevertheless, the distinctiveness of Sor Juana, of her personality as well as her work, is the most pronounced. . . . Her case is unique."

Not only her illegitimate birth and withdrawal from the world into a religious order, Paz argues, but the special isolation conferred by her historical context—in the period of the Spanish Empire's decline, in a place remote from the European cultural capitals of the age, the New World city of Mexico—make her case unique. It was an event of genius occurring very much against the grain of a society in which, as Paz emphasizes, the subjugation of women was total, and "neither the word nor the concept [of feminism] existed."

The available information out of which Paz elaborates his story of Juana's solitary struggle can be covered in a few lines. The out-of-wedlock daughter of a Spanish-Basque captain and an unmarried, self-reliant farm manageress, Juana, at fifteen, becomes by virtue of her beauty and brilliance the favorite maid-in-waiting and protégée of the vicereine at the colonial court in Mexico City.

Prevented by her sex from attending university, and from finding a suitable match by the circumstances of her birth and what she calls "my total disinclination to marriage," five years later she turns her back on secular pleasures for a life of literary and intellectual pursuits inside a convent.

For the next two decades she writes the poems and verse-plays that win her renown as the "Phoenix of Mexico." But Juana's poetry continues to retain more of the redolent artifice of the court than the rigorous asperity of the cloister, and in the end religious authorities, increasingly disapproving of its wide circulation and envious of her growing fame, pressure her to abjure her writing.

The independent Juana finds herself up against a formidable lineup of male foes, among them her confessor, an Inquisition censor, and the archbishop of Mexico, a violent misogynist. She submits, and after two years of silence and self-mortification, dies of plague in 1695, in her mid-forties.

It's impossible to miss Paz's sympathetic involvement in his story, his instinctive identification with the plight of the dissenting creative spirit in a closed society controlled by an omnipotent bureaucracy "governing in the name of orthodoxy."

Differing from Catholic critics who have seen Juana's final renunciation of her art as a triumph of faith, Paz views it as a parabolic historical tragedy, the necessary fate of the artist cornered by orthodoxy. "My generation saw the revolutionaries of 1917, the comrades of Lenin and Trotsky, confess false crimes before their judges in a language that was an abject parody of Marxism, just as the sanctimonious language of the affirmations of faith Sor Juana signed with her blood is a caricature of religious language."

Up against this spurious language of oppression, Paz champions that of the mind freely seeking truth. His most eloquent passages respond to the note of passionate philosophical inquiry in Juana's writings—he compares "First Dream," her long poem about a "reality seen not by the senses but by the soul," with the attempts of moderns such as Mallarmé to image the solitary soul confronting an open universe—and to her lifelong devotion to her books and studies.

The power of her love of learning, indeed, is the most striking element in Paz's multidimensional portrait of Sor Juana. Drinking in the "mother's milk" of reading, contemplating one's soul mirrored in a starry sky "or its double, the page"—these things, Paz tells us with the weight of his own half-century of literary experience underpinning his conjecture about this mystery woman of three centuries ago, "will not undo the knot of fate, but can at least help us understand our condition."

Sor Juana is a huge, magnificent poetic constellation of a book.

Translator Alan Trueblood has followed Paz's tips in compiling an important companion volume to the biography: the bilingual *Sor Juana Anthology*, providing the English-only reader a look at the best of Juana's poetic work (as well as her "Reply to Sor Philothea," an impassioned prose defense of her calling as a writer).

Given the difficulties of translating stylized seventeenth-century meters and conceits, Trueblood's versions seem to transmit much of the intricate "design, proportion, clarity, gracefulness, self-awareness, irony, lucidity" that her eminent biographer finds in the Mexican nun's poetry.

With remarkable accuracy, the verse reflects the major themes of the life as conveyed by Paz; behind the indirection of the baroque metaphysical conceits, the emotional and spiritual urgencies of Juana's complicated existence stand revealed. One sonnet, for instance, obliquely considers her isolated existence in the religious order and the perils of "a way of life binding a whole life through." Another, titled "She shows distress at being abused for the applause her talent brings," begins "Fate, was my crime of such enormity. . . ."

More than a mere ornament to Paz's massive biography, Sor Juana's intellectual rebellion in poetry must be digested to fully understand the true nature and dimensions of this dialogue of affinity across the centuries and the sexes between two of Mexico's greatest writers.

Iberian Roots

A young lawyer and successful writer of novels and stories with six fiction books to his credit by the time of the outbreak of the Spanish Civil War, Salvador Espriu observed the revolutionary upheaval in Barcelona, the bombardment, assassinations, persecution, deaths of friends and family. "All I know," he would write years after this prolonged, irreversible chain of shocks, "is that / blood I did not shed / has wrecked the world."

The work of this greatest of modern Catalonian poets, now appearing in *Selected Poems of Salvador Espriu,* has not taken this long to reach English by accident. The poet himself, who died in 1985, did little to press his poems upon the world, partly out of necessity.

"The strange time entered me / in jails of silence." Following Franco's victory, Espriu's beloved Catalan language was officially proscribed, forbidden in schools, books, newspapers, magazines and even public conversations, making mere utterance into an act of defiance. When the ban was lifted in 1946, Espriu ended a period of mute witness and re-emerged as a writer, but one transformed, having now abandoned his stories and "turned"—his translator says in her preface—"to poetry almost as a monk to prayer."

The poems incorporated a new tragic-elegiac vision, memorializing "my dead moving off / one by one down long / rows of silence," marking with fatalistic sadness "the closed dance

Review of *Selected Poems of Salvador Espriu,* translated by Magda Bogin; *Late and Posthumous Poems: 1968–1974* by Pablo Neruda, translated by Ben Belitt; and *Rhythm, Content & Flavor* by Victor Hernandez Cruz, *San Francisco Chronicle,* 1989.

of everyone" left among the living, yet also keeping up the small flame of a redemptive dream, the lingering "whole yearning / for salvation" of his native country. "When someone asks / What keeps you / in this harsh, arid, / blood soaked land? / Surely it is not / the best land you could find," he wrote in one poem, "We answer simply, / in our dream it is."

He managed to maintain a low-profile legal career, escaping, in physical terms at least, the Falangist police reprisals suffered by many of his fellow Catalonian patriots. His own long trials were largely internalized, his poetry becoming his clandestine shelter and refuge from the terror around him.

In the covert coded language of his poems, his own generation of young Spaniards became lost souls, people of the "Golah" (Hebrew term for the diaspora) while the wounded motherland, Spain itself, became "Sepharad" (again a Hebraic name, recalling the sufferings of an earlier exodus, that of the Sephardim in the fifteenth century). And the central mythic ground of his poetry was also a place half real, half symbolic—the tiny fishing village of Arenys, just up the coast from Barcelona, where the poet's parents were born, where he spent his childhood (and now lies buried). This ancestral spiritual home, functioning in his poetry as what the Greeks called *temenos*, or sacred precinct, is given the anagrammatic name "Sinera"; its spare landscape of sea, sky, rock, hill and vine contribute the source-images of his writing.

Mined, shaped and polished from the stark, dramatic monosyllables of the Catalan tongue—that mysterious "gold" as Espriu called it, into which he'd plunged his artist's hands—the poems inscribe an elemental and basic lexicon, recalling the narrow, emotionally charged vocabularies of mystics or displaced persons. "I chose the simplest / words to tell myself," Espriu says in one poem. On his solitary castaway's "naked rock of song," each word counts.

> From the sea I will be saved
> perhaps, by poetry, a few
> bright words that stand
> for my whole life.
>
> ("Diptych for the Living")

A valuable introduction by Espriu's longtime friend and publisher Francesc Vallverdú informs us the poet spent his last twenty years more or less withdrawn from the world, a virtual recluse living out his "high conception of literature" by committing himself to his poetic canticle, designed, as one verse proclaimed, to "give each thing a final name / as old memory shapes new creation." Unpretentious about his intent, Espriu modestly considered his art "a small help in living an upright life and perhaps in dying a good death." Though political conflict and its aftermath indelibly stamped his poetry's course, the deeper attitude the poems ultimately convey is as Vallverdú suggests "not so much political as . . . 'prophetic' in the Hebraic tradition."

One of Espriu's best poems is an homage to the great Chilean poet Pablo Neruda, consciously echoing the latter's more flamboyant style to acknowledge a fellowship in art and resistance, and hailing a future where "we shall be freed forever / from the wells dug by long fear."

Neruda's own *Late and Posthumous Poems: 1968–1974*, a bilingual edition like the Espriu book, brings over into English a good sample of the large body of work he left behind upon his death in 1973. Eight separate Spanish-language volumes, most of them posthumous, are represented here.

It is Neruda's swan song. Terminally ill in these years, spending much of his time alone in his oceanside retreat at Isla Negra, he continued to shoulder the heavy public burden of his position as world man and world poet—a campaign of his own for president of Chile on the Communist party ticket, followed by extensive travels to support the candidacy of Allende, the ambassadorship to France, a Nobel Prize and then a recurrence of cancer in Paris.

This is a contemplative, even rueful Neruda, addressing megalithic Easter Island figures as sad, wise peers—"O lone, pensive dignitaries." In "Child of the Moon" the humble railroad worker's son mourns his narrow, alienating calling as a word-maker—"I feel the world never belonged to me." "A Heavy Surf," one of many poems which the ubiquitous sea dominates as a symbol of infinite duration up against man's extremely short-term existence, closes on a gesture of surren-

der to cosmic inevitability: "Then when the wind has had its
way with us / we can see ourselves as we are, face to face with
the invisible." And in "One Comes Back"—a poem of his last
months—he confronts the transitoriness of his own identity in
a voice that is, like much of the best of his work, universal:

> One comes back to the I, the old house
> with its nails and interstices, yes,
> to a selfhood grown bored with its selfhood,
> a suit full of holes; one
> tries to walk naked in rain,
> a man wants to wet himself down in clean water, in
> elementary wind, but gets only
> as far as the well of his selfhood again,
> the old, piddling obsessions:
> did I really exist? did I know what to say,
> or to pay or to owe or discover?
> —as if my importance were such
> that the world with its vegetal name,
> its black-walled arena,
> had no choice but to accept or deny me.

Victor Hernandez Cruz is an American poet of Iberian
roots several times removed—transplanted from the Caribbean to New York's Lower East Side and then to the San
Francisco Bay, he has followed his poetry all the way back to
his sources. "I walked in Puerto Rico with a guitar in my
belly / I walked in Spain with Mecca / in my sandals . . . / I
walk in New York with a fan / in my pocket / made with the
feathers of / three continents. . . ."

Rhythm, Content & Flavor traces the progression of Cruz's
work through highlights of four previously published volumes, from early documents of youth in the "crazy city" of
New York ("Your whip is so strong / Not all can walk your line
/ We walk it with our hands / And survive like seashell neck-
laces") to a recent sequence titled "Atlantis: The Age of Sea-
shells," recounting his belated homecoming to the island culture of his birthplace. "That imaginary place / called Puerto
Rico" here flowers into lyric myth, as a lost continent of
paradisal poetry and vivid music, "sound surrounded by wa-

ter / Islands of green pensivity / Going and coming rock eternity / We could say the fish started here."

Cruz's main subject is the power of poetry and music to transform. The movement in his verse is from music to knowledge to myth, but it all starts from the music, a seamless bilingual lyricism weaving tongues, beats and accents, salsa, bop and soul into a "Manhattan dance Latin / in Spanish to African rhythms / A language lesson / Without opening your mouth."

One True Word beyond Betrayal

Third-generation Japanese-American writer David Mura's disparate cultural roots are the source of much generative tension in his notable first book of poems, *After We Lost Our Way*.

Mura's Asian background absorbs him, both as literal "familial inheritance"—in poems about the struggles of his immigrant grandparents, inmates of a World War II relocation camp, and of his *nisei* father, a GI in the Philippines during the war—and as sympathetic affinity. In a search for "one true word beyond / betrayal," he takes up as subjects the vast legions of the historically betrayed: the *hibakushas* (atomic bomb survivors), the Japanese-American "relocation" victims of the Second War, and the post-Vietnam waves of refugees to America from Southeast Asia. The long shadow of racism and imperialist aggression lays heavy across these pages.

Yet as a *sansei* who grew up and still lives in the Midwest, Mura is never able to view the Asian/American interface without seeing things from both sides at once. Nor, as a male raised in and thoroughly suffused with the effects of the white man's patriarchal culture, is he able to deny a troubling psychic identification with the aggressor as well as the victim in history. A poem about pornography called "The Bookstore" is a chilling document of male sexual addiction.

The theme of "libidinous desire for dominance" is taken up again elsewhere, most memorably in the course of a deceptively casual meditation on the poet's thorny relations with his wife's Yankee antecedents. A poem whose long, sinuous lines

---

Review of *After We Lost Our Way* by David Mura, *San Francisco Chronicle*, 1989.

unfold not only a tale of external-world events but the ceaseless narrative of inner history, "Grandfather-in-Law" moves by surprising leaps of insight from bitterly observed cultural irony and controlled anger through agonized self-examination to final forgiveness, arriving at an unexpected yet beautifully earned embracing of contraries in which both wounded self and WASP in-laws find sympathy and acknowledgment.

This serious, gifted young writer's crazy-quilt of influences is well symbolized by the sixteenth-century Japanese patchwork coat he's chosen to adorn the jacket of his book. There are traces of the American mainstream poetic modes (Wright, Levine, Dickey) in which he was obviously educated, but these are by no means definitive or limiting. Though long isolated (except in imagination) from his Eastern Pacific Rim genetic sources, Mura seems to return to them in his hauntingly open endings. These poems don't so much close as hang in space on held pauses of thought: the effect is a ghostly evanescence of feeling not unreminiscent of the stillness of haiku, Issa's infinite world of dew.

Mura's eclecticism gives the work layering and dimension. His poetic experiments with narrative voice, setting and magic realism show the imprint less of other poets than of prose artists like Faulkner, Woolf, Duras, Marquez. His ironic attention to history points back to extensive European philosophical influences—Benjamin, Adorno, Canetti, Barthes. And in a sequence on the life of the persecuted Italian artist-genius Pier Paolo Pasolini he applies up-to-date techniques of psychological biography to construct a parable of "individual grief" in a "self-consumed time."

Mura's reverberating theme is the cruelty and irony of history, the endless repetition of its mocking, insistent metaphors. His poetry offers a curing of all that pain through hope captured in fleeting but redemptive images of harmony in creation.

Whispered Secrets

I know very little about Killarney Clary beyond the fact that this slender first book's fifty-four startling, unsettling prose poems—at once offhand and evocatively compelling, oblique and eerily familiar, intimate and mysteriously elusive—vault her into some rarefied company. Baudelaire and Rimbaud come to mind, Pierre Reverdy, Max Jacob. To my way of thinking no writer in English has ever done more breathtaking things with the prose-poem form than this unheralded newcomer from, of all unlikely places, Pasadena.

The immediate locations in *Who Whispered Near Me* are as mundane as everyday American middle-class existence: the beaches, freeways, business offices and residential streets of that vast "Inland Empire" cradled between Southern California's ocean and mountains, desert and shore. But in Clary's hands this setting, otherwise routine as any television series backdrop, becomes a dreamscape of improbable urgency, its tight commuter lanes and landlocked surburban driveways transformed into evanescent meditative spaces, ephemeral locales of desire and longing, yearning and sadness, aching grief and a detachment discovered beyond thoughts of death in "a way to let go of senses."

Memorized static perspectives give way to a world of moving, buoyant surfaces, animated by "swells of kelp, of cloud, of leaves in the new wind from Palm Springs, of ochre dust on the dry edge of idleness." Through cleansed vision Clary glimpses a personal history rendered as freshly as some newly

Review of *Who Whispered Near Me* by Killarney Clary, *San Francisco Chronicle*, 1989.

discovered natural process: "I floated the way a heart floats in the body, the way life is buoyed by the blood without difficulty or rest."

If there is dislocation, distortion and displacement in this vision, there is also a surprising closeness of contact. This is a writer whose direct, confidential emotional address constantly shocks, challenges and engages. "Confidant, do we place our trust here, deep in the heart of trouble?" Clary invites us into an intimate world peopled by friends, familiars, loved ones living and dead, whose common names—Sarah, Mary Lou, Helen, Kathleen, Anne, Billy, Ralph—are inscribed like mysterious landmarks. Keeping few secrets, she nevertheless resists being pinned down by her revelations into predictability. Hers is a story thread never quite completed. "I will tell you everything, but now, habitually, I am leaving."

The result is a constant reminding of just how variable and volatile are the actual unfoldings of feeling, once exposed in their genuine light. Perpetually in quest of "solutions," Clary is at the same time resigned to their unattainability. "I talk all day about escrow and interest. I drive a long way home and each time I start out feeling one way and arrive feeling the opposite. Resolutions are worthless in this swamp." "Nothing ends, nothing takes us back, forgives, repairs."

The unexpected response is the only thing truly expectable from one page to the next of this book. Clary's greatest strength as a writer is a generous openness of spirit. That sympathetic receptiveness to experience, to a domain of process and plenitude whose "fortune opens [a] surface which is, after all, beauty," reflects an uncanny ability to go out of self and into the other, an identifying capacity allowing unique penetration of person, thing and place without disturbance of natural clarities. Removing distances between writer and reader, subject and object, Killarney Clary returns us to that realm of the "ordinary, spectacular" in which we've always lived without recognizing it.

"Out there in the calm, exposed, I might look back toward home. Everything, everyone is out of place, moving or turning again, able to see both sides of any argument. And I am there. Onshore, a woman sweeps her toddler off to the parking lot for reasons weak and distant to me; but I understand—some discomfort or foreboding, fatigue from blowing sand or the glare, or maybe tired joy. I drift away from the determined ones on solid ground. And I am there."

Death's Duties

Raymond Carver, acclaimed poet and writer of short fiction, died of cancer in 1988 at the age of fifty. An accomplished storyteller, Carver throughout his work consistently employed straightforward narrative modes to engage universal themes of love, doubt and fear, themes objectified in everyday images and situations of a commonness betraying his own democratic instincts and working-class background. *A New Path to the Waterfall* brings that work to an appropriate if painful close. In these agonizingly naked, direct last verses, addressing that most universal of all themes, the inexorable encroachment of mortality, Carver attempted to conjoin his own words side by side with those of a literary ancestor in many respects his similar, Anton Chekhov.

Consciously playing off his poems against passages from Chekhov's clear, simple prose tales of peasant life by intermingling the two in such a way as to suggest affinities of mood, feeling and spirit, Carver seems to have been not only asserting an elective literary identification but also perhaps sensing a need to somehow control and formalize the outpouring of his own grief through a bonding with the considerably more distanced writings of the Russian realist master. (And it is not just the work of Chekhov, but that of other writers—including whole poems by Jaroslav Seifert, Tomas Tranströmer, Czeslaw Milosz—which Carver interspersed among his poems to arrive at this unusual anthology-patchwork structure, with a

Review of *A New Path to the Waterfall* by Raymond Carver, with an Introduction by Tess Gallagher, *San Francisco Chronicle,* 1989.

ratio of only two Carver pieces to each one by his "guest" authors.)

The distancing effort, if indeed that's what it's to be taken as, sometimes works effectively, creating a sense of real integration, the disparate voices joining spirits in a single anthem of lamentation and loss; at other times one feels Carver, understandably overcome by personal distress and the pressure of precious time escaping him ("I've got," he blurts at one point, "how much longer?"), merely succumbing to the facts of life and its leave-taking, and making do, desperately pulling a book together out of whatever lies at hand, right down to extended quotes from old angler's manuals and random notes found in his bathrobe pocket.

Ultimately, the rather heroic attempt at distancing by juxtaposition collapses before the wrenching verisimilitude of death's duties. The book has an awful inevitability of structure about it. A fine storyteller to the end, Carver takes his reader on a final journey that leads in one direction, downward into darkness.

Never a writer much given to mediation, he moves here from the comparatively shapely, artful and well-honed "revived" early love poems in an opening section through increasing degrees of confessional immersion in suffering, from woes and trials of early childhood family experiences through pains of a bad early marriage and a mid-life period of alcoholism before arriving in the later sections at his fearsome wrestling match to the finish with what Joseph Conrad once called the destructive element, embodied in the form of an advancing cancer in lung and brain. "Apprehension, and then, then stupendous / grief" take over as the last poems describe a horrific game of tag with death itself, played out from page to page with few emotional changes left unwrung right down to the predictable reluctant, clinging surrender.

This is, then, a unique book, one whose plainnesses and tensions are to be experienced not formally but emotionally, as one listens to a children's story about mysterious happenings in the dark or says a prayer in the middle of the night, reads a goodbye note from a loved one or hears the cry of a terribly wounded animal. Its confessional pathos, narrowed to a fine point like the sadly ironic "jaunty slant" of a cigarette in the poet's mouth noticed in an old photograph, is at once oppressive and moving, and is relieved only in a small coda called "Last Fragment," hinting redemptively at acceptance after all that grief. "And did you get what / you wanted from this life, even so? / I did. / And what did you want? / To call myself beloved, to feel myself / beloved on the earth."

Salutary Pessimism in an
Administered World

In a period of depressing predictability and sameness in almost all sectors of the English-speaking poetry scene, the publication, three years posthumously, of British poet Philip Larkin's *Collected Poems* is an event of real magnitude.

Larkin, as this book ought to prove to anyone who still doubted it, was not only a good but a great poet, one whose wry, disaffected yet oddly salutary pessimism comes to feel more and more timely and tonic, if not also prophetic, with the years.

The dominant note of feeling in the poetry we find here is one of sadness, or to use Larkin's own words, of a "sometimes gentle, sometimes ironic, sometimes bitter, but always passive apprehension of suffering" which came to him both naturally and by way of his chief influence and the poet he most resembles, Thomas Hardy.

An earlier influence of Larkin's youth, much evident in the juvenilia relegated to the rear of this book by editor Anthony Thwaite, was W. B. Yeats, who once commented that "passive suffering is not a theme for poetry." Larkin, in an essay, responded caustically that the Celtic bard's remark had been "fatuous." The evidence of Larkin's own verse—much amplified in this *Collected*, which contains some 130 poems not included by the fastidious poet in the four slim volumes he

---

Review of *Collected Poems* by Philip Larkin, edited with an Introduction by Anthony Thwaite, *San Francisco Chronicle*, 1989.

chose to publish in his lifetime—is certainly proof of the truth of that retort.

It is Larkin's acute apprehension of passive suffering which makes his poetry, for all its rhyming and scanning and other reactionary surface tendencies—reflection, in technical terms, of certain of his social attitudes—so surprisingly relevant to the administered world of the present moment.

For where there are passive victims, there are Larkin themes. The unhappy condition of the institutionalized ill and elderly in Britain's welfare state, for instance, is a subject more than once circled back to here, as in the 1961 "Ambulances" ("Far / From the exchange of love to lie / Unreachable inside a room / The traffic parts to let go by"); or in the previously uncollected 1972 "Heads In the Women's Ward," which soon leads, as this edition's useful chronological rearrangement of the poems shows, to a superior effort on the same theme, "The Old Fools." (Here as elsewhere, the new order of poems enables us to see the neurotic-perfectionist poet playing with and worrying over his subjects until at last they yield a fully realized work.)

In Larkin even death itself—final cog in "the unbeatable slow machine / That brings what you get"—is mechanical and administered. Another of this book's eighty or so uncollected (post-1945) mature pieces, and the most complex and accomplished of them, the 1977 "Aubade," is a hyper-gloomy middle-of-the-night meditation on "the dread of dying, and being dead." This poem elevates Larkin's congenital morbidity to new imaginative levels, eventually vanishing into a chilly administrative image: "postmen like doctors go from house to house."

"Deceptions," part of a 1950 burst in which, as one sees here, a Larkin still shy of thirty left tentative starts behind and grasped in one prolonged rush the tougher, darker voice of his mature work, is at once a poem specifically about rape and sexual violence, and a statement of the metaphorical relation joining the victims of such crimes with all passive sufferers in an administered world. Its occasion is the forcible "ruining" of a poor London slum girl of the early industrial era. "I would not dare / console you if I could," the poet tells the long-departed victim.

> For you would hardly care
> That you were less deceived, out on that bed
> Than he was, stumbling up the breathless stair
> To burst into fulfillment's desolate attic.

There are no more youthful illusions in the poems following that one, and especially not in those confronting contemporary sexuality. Shy, reclusive bachelor librarian Larkin wrote little romantic verse after his poetic apprenticeship. "Love Again," a previously unpublished 1979 piece, seeks out a realistic definition of modern love in the clinical language of the scientific researcher:

> Isolate rather this element
>
> That sways them on in a sort of sense
> And say it never worked for me.
> Something to do with violence
> A long way back, and wrong rewards
> And arrogant eternity.

Larkin's apprehension of passive suffering extends outward from the human to the animal world, where the specter of domination that haunts his verse finds perhaps its purest victims. The uncollected 1979 "The Mower," an ironic variation on a theme of Andrew Marvell (whom Larkin revered as a onetime fellow resident of the provincial town of Hull), mourns a hedgehog caught in the poet's lawnmower—but with a characteristically Larkinesque refusal of sentimentality: "Now I had mauled its unobtrusive world / Unmendably. Burial was no help: / Next morning I got up and it did not." Even more to the point is the unpublished 1965 "Ape Experiment Room," surely an example of the kind of "naked" or "raw" poem which, Thwaite suggests, Larkin often held back from publication. Administrative cruelty is once again the central motif, with the amorality of institutional lab researchers— "putting questions to flesh / That no one would think to ask"—placed in tension against the mute suffering of the creatures they torture. This is a poem with all the moral gravity, if not the polished finish, of Larkin's finest.

A grimly witty note, it should be said, is never completely absent from this poet's voice, and his satires, especially those aimed at himself, become increasingly acerbic—and funny— in the few poems he wrote in his later years. Those major pieces which won him the literary fame and publicity he abhorred and shunned—"The Whitsun Weddings," "Church Going," "High Windows," "Dockery and Son"—are all of course here, and they are as great as ever, but a poem we might now remember Larkin just as accurately by is another of those withheld later pieces, the unpublished 1978 "The Winter Palace."

This short poem, whose spareness, clarity and merciless candor are trademarks of the propositional style Larkin came to just before running dry as a poet in the last years of his life, is a self-mocking admission of personal regression ("Most people know more as they get older: / I give all that the cold shoulder") which comes down to a familiar Larkin image, one of floating away into vacancy and nothingness. The isolated redemptive moments of his poetry bring all the planet's lonely and sad consciousness-sufferers similar prospects of ultimate release.

> It will be worth it, if in the end I manage
> To blank out whatever it is that is doing the damage.
>
> Then there will be nothing I know.
> My mind will fold into itself, like snow.

Lost Dreams

This book continues what its editor, Robert Phillips, calls a "rescue mission": retrieving the uncollected and unpublished poems of Delmore Schwartz, and at the same time resuscitating Schwartz's literary stock, which has not exactly been soaring of late. To an original version of this book issued ten years ago, Phillips now adds sixteen recently discovered poems as well as a selection from Schwartz's ill-fated early 1940s stab at a master-opus in verse, "Genesis," out of print for nearly four decades.

A Freudian reading of the Jewish identity struggle as seen through Biblical, personal and world history, the never-completed "Genesis," we're able to see from this fragment, is full of fine lines but also excessively rhetorical, diffuse, euphonious and long-winded. While it was in progress, the poet excitedly predicted his epic would "last as long as the Pyramids." Its failure signaled the beginning of the end for his poetry.

Last & Lost charts Schwartz's declension from the awesome poet he was in his early twenties—the most prodigiously gifted as well as the most advanced in career terms of a generation that included his friends John Berryman and Robert Lowell—to the writer of windy, exhilarated doggerel we find in the late poems here ("O the brio, & presto, & allegro . . . so furious: so joyous: so spontaneous").

"All dreams come true." By the time he wrote that line from "Genesis," Schwartz, an overachiever who spent his adulthood overcoming the insecurity of a Depression child-

---

Review of *Last & Lost Poems* by Delmore Schwartz, edited by Robert Phillips, *San Francisco Chronicle*, 1989.

hood in a middle-class Jewish immigrant family, had already grasped a large share of his own dreams. Those dreams were all along conditioned by Hollywood movies (or as Schwartz lovingly termed them in his journals, "moon pictures"). He never got over his romance with Hollywood's star-images and the Narcissus-like quality of film watching; the "flashback of the cinema, / fadeout, dissolve, return" fascinated him as a kind of imitation of consciousness, a fable of real life.

The above quotes from "Genesis" are echoed in other early "lost" pieces. The two finest poems in this book are taut, brilliant mementos of the Baudelairean Schwartz style of 1937 titled "Metro-Goldwyn-Mayer" and "You, My Photographer." Both register sensitive, ironic recognition of the coming role of visual media, especially film, in American life. "I looked toward the movie, the common dream," Schwartz begins the former poem.

He had an uncanny way with first lines and titles. A recycled Yeats line he chose as the title of his 1938 debut collection, *In Dreams Begin Responsibilities*, proved prophetic. With Wallace Stevens's *Harmonium*, the book still ranks as one of the two most accomplished first volumes of poetry ever written in this country. Upon its publication, Schwartz was appointed by critics in the major reviews as poetic spokesman of an entire uncertain, disillusioned East Coast intellectual generation. Irving Howe called him "the poet of the historical moment."

His effort to remain so drove Schwartz into a fury to keep current; he quoted the latest German philosophers in "Genesis," and in another "rescued" early work here, vowed earnestly to "follow thought and what the world announces." It was an effort that led him into the narrow confines of a mainstream writing and teaching career, and ended in competitiveness, disappointment, alcoholism, chemical abuse, paranoia, manic depression and a too-early dissolution of skills. To anyone familiar with that disturbing emblem which was Schwartz's life, the euphoric organ music of his last poems is likely to sound painfully hollow, the racket of a mind coming apart at the peaks of what Schwartz once called his "manic-depressive roller-coaster."

That "tone and chant of rapture, supreme and surpassing all," which the poet strains mightily to hear in a late and lengthy effusion titled "Overture," in truth sounds only once in the later selections in this book—in a series of translations done in the early 1960s. Restrained from his free verse flights by the disciplines of translation, Schwartz produced inspired versions of two Paul Valéry poems: "To Helen," and a passage from "The Graveyard By the Sea." These do indeed manage the elusive, ecstatic note Delmore was always willing to consume himself to hit: "Time itself sparkles, to dream and to know are one . . . ."

Moving toward Annihilation

Wearing his troubled psyche on his sleeve like a perverse badge of honor, John Berryman turned the purgatories of personal history into a poetry of brilliant black-comic desperation. His traumatic childhood marked by the suicide of his father, and the lifelong shame and loss which ensued from that event; his catastrophic alcoholism, several ruined marriages, and endless agitated combat with private demons; his late, willful attempt at religious conversion, short-circuited by the taking of his own life in the midst of great fame at the age of fifty-seven—all these trials save the last became fuel for his verse. (And even his suicide was also fodder, in that his obsessive anticipating of it provided him many haunting poems.) The *Collected Poems 1937–1971* is evidence of the presence of a rare lyric gift in among all those neurotic symptoms and manic intensities.

This was a writer who saw the life of the artist as a continual "moving towards annihilation—towards becoming a voice." The voice he made of himself—jagged, jumpy, nervously angular, self-consciously idiosyncratic in syntax and idiom—is one that will not soon be forgotten.

Berryman's later work—especially the final volumes collected here, the 1971 *Love & Fame* and the posthumously published *Delusions, etc.* (1972)—is chilling testament of a long, compulsive descent into self-destruction, with the pursuit of literary glory as its ironic subtext. Though he bemoaned the "almost insuperable difficulty of writing high

---

Review of *John Berryman: Collected Poems 1937–1971,* edited and introduced by Charles Thornbury, *San Francisco Chronicle,* 1989.

verse in a land that cared and cares so little for it," in fact no poet of this land has ever accumulated such sheer weight of laurels (we're talking Pulitzer, Bollingen, Guggenheim, National Book Award, just for starters) as did Berryman in his last years. An ability to manipulate the voyeuristic national craving for emotional self-exposure even while suffering through the dark nights of his soul was not least among his many talents.

A sophisticated scholar and critic as well as poet, Berryman possessed a special consciousness of our verse heritage. Apart from the protracted autobiographical epic *Dream Songs* (which is regrettably not included here), his most impressive attempt at a self-contained long work was the carefully researched 1953 "Homage to Mistress Bradstreet."

The fifty-seven stanza "Homage" takes the form of an extended dramatic dialogue with Anne Bradstreet, a high-minded seventeenth-century New England Puritan woman who as Berryman wryly observed, "may have been our first American poet but is not a good one." It is at once a peculiar long-distance love poem ("I fell in love with her," he later confessed, "and wrote about her, putting myself in it . . . it was a sort of extended witch-seductress and demon-lover bit") and an affecting statement of sympathetic affinity ("I did not choose her, somehow she chose me"). In what he perceived as their common condition of isolated aristocratic sensibility confronting a harsh and unreceptive environment, the contemporary poet found a surprisingly solid basis for this unlikely ecstatic bonding. "We are on each other's hands / who care," he exclaims to Anne at one point, as though neither had anyone else. "Homage" remains a curious and moving experiment, still arresting in its urgent, expressive gesturing across barriers of gender, culture and history.

Anne Bradstreet's personal battle between rebellion and submission in "Homage" parallels a conflict in Berryman's own poetic development. On the level of style, this conflict was manifest as a struggle between the gestural immediacy that came most naturally to him and the rhetorical restraint which was his reaction against it.

The latter quality of formality and control dominated his

earliest mature work, of which the pivot and touchstone remains the masterly 1939 "Winter Landscape," first evidence that youthful influences of Yeats and Auden were about to yield to an original voice. This ominously somber piece, based on Breughel's painting *Hunters in the Snow*, is as Berryman once said, "a war-poem of an unusual negative kind," its emblematic figures trudging wearily into "evil history" suggestive not merely of hunters but of Hitler's brownshirts, the "poles" upon their shoulders not only spears but guns. The poem's strength is its extreme understatement, its impact contained in a deliberately missing or misrepresented element—what the poet obliquely signals but carefully does *not* say about a violent world.

The consummate poise and sober restraint would give way over the years to a quirky, whistling-in-the-dark jocularity, as Berryman's poetry increasingly both tempted fate and courted his own demise. His own "life-suffering & pure heart / & hardly definable but central weaknesses" became his relentless concentration, in verse that painfully invested the whole world with self and was relieved only by a dark self-mocking humor.

In the end the tensions in the work grew less and less mediated. He observed in an interview that "some of the best kind of writing is really transparent . . . you get no impression of viewing art." That became his own final artistic goal, achieved here and there in the terrifying compulsive candor of late poems like "Of Suicide" and "Henry's Understanding," where the glance toward doom is less sidelong and oblique than direct and frontal.

"Reflexions on suicide, & on my father, possess me," the former boldly opens. "I drink too much, my wife threatens separation . . . ." The poem's cool, matter-of-fact tonality is a thin disguise over the horrors, its primary emotional effect a chilling shiver, a sense of watching someone dare himself to take that final dive.

"Henry's Understanding" adopts, then quickly sheds, the persona of *Dream Songs*, betraying how little patience the poet had left by this time for disguises; the "he" of the first line has become "I" by the fourth, as understanding grows. The poem describes a suicide impulse experienced some twenty-five years earlier, in a vacation house on the coast of Maine—an urge to rise from bed, strip, enter "the terrible water & walk forever / under it toward the island."

It is impossible now to read such lines without remembering that within months of writing them Berryman had plunged to his death from a bridge over the Mississippi River. His verse had finally achieved that perfect transparency, becoming less poetry than talisman, and providing the reader little impression of viewing art, so vivid and immediate was the life-agony implied. One only hopes that after all his tribulations, Berryman found that island.

UNDER DISCUSSION
Donald Hall, General Editor

Volumes in the Under Discussion series collect reviews and essays about individual poets. The series is concerned with contemporary American and English poets about whom the consensus has not yet been formed and the final vote has not been taken. Titles in the series include:

Elizabeth Bishop and Her Art
edited by Lloyd Schwartz and Sybil P. Estess
Richard Wilbur's Creation
edited and with an Introduction by Wendy Salinger
Reading Adrienne Rich
edited by Jane Roberta Cooper
On the Poetry of Allen Ginsberg
edited by Lewis Hyde
Robert Bly: When Sleepers Awake
edited by Joyce Peseroff
Robert Creeley's Life and Work
edited by John Wilson
On the Poetry of Galway Kinnell
edited by Howard Nelson
On Louis Simpson
edited by Hank Lazer
Anne Sexton
edited by Steven E. Colburn
James Wright
edited by Peter Stitt and Frank Graziano
Frank O'Hara
edited by Jim Elledge

Forthcoming volumes will examine the work of Langston Hughes, Philip Levine, Muriel Rukeyser, H.D., and Denise Levertov, among others.

Please write for further information on available editions and current prices.

Ann Arbor **The University of Michigan Press**